God c

Do infinitely more than we ever dare ask or imagine

A Housewife's Extraordinary Journey with Jesus

MIRACLES, SIGNS &WONDERS!

Tanya Lord

Miracles are God's way of showing us He is here!

Kingdom Publishers

www.kingdompublishers.co.uk

God Can Do Infinitely More Than We Ever Dare Ask or Imagine! - A Housewife's Extraordinary Journey with Jesus

All Scripture Quotations have been taken from the Passion Translation, the New International Version, Amplified Version, the New Living Translation and the Message Translation.

ISBN: 978-1-911697-27-5

1st Edition by Kingdom Publishers
Kingdom Publishers
London, UK.

You can purchase copies of this book from any leading bookstore or email contact@kingdompublishers.co.uk

Miracles are God's way of showing us He is here!

Contents

Miracles are God's way of showing us He is here!

Acknowledgments & Dedication

"Every little miracle points to our Heavenly Father"

I give all the thanks and praise to my Heavenly Father for all He has done. Without the power, and help of His Holy Spirit, none of this would have been possible. Let me explain.

Early one Sunday morning before church, when my husband was recovering in the tropical disease unit in hospital, the Holy Spirit inspired me to write this book. Giving me not only the ideas, but the detail of every chapter, and who the book was to be written for. Also before I was even aware of Kingdom Publishers, I was praying for the perfect publisher and the Holy Spirit gave me a picture of a crown which I now know is the logo of the publishers of this book – Kingdom Publishers. I stand amazed, honoured, and so thrilled to be invited to write this book; My prayer is that you will be inspired and it will be a blessing to all those that read it, and all who give it away, as a gift to others to read.

To my wonderful Husband, our amazing daughter and family. I love you so much from the bottom of my heart, thank you for everything for your endless encouragement and love. Thank you for inviting me to be your wife and for everything you do and have done, and for enabling me to be able to write this book.

To my lovely parents I love you also so much, all my amazing friends (there are so many of you!), prayer partners Lois, Sarah and Julia, Ablaze Prayer team at St Nic's Nottingham, and the Worship Team at Holy Trinity Church Leicester, and to everyone who has ever prayed. Thank you, I could not have done this without you. I am so blessed, and so grateful for your friendship, love and encouragement. You are all just the best, and such an inspiration to me in the way you live your lives, and your love for Jesus. Thank you for all your prayers, so much of all that has happened, is because, you have also believed, and asked God, for these miracles too. Thank You!

Forward

Dear potential reader of this book. I don't know where you are on your spiritual journey……. whether you are at a place of searching or have been a believer for some time. I want to say there is something here for you to enjoy and be stimulated by.

Tanya in her writing grasps so well, in a way so few writers today seem to express, how much God loves us, longs for us to share in that love through answered prayer and the kind of relationship we can have with Him. She illustrates this through her words and her own life experiences.

Her writing gently invites us to share in God's love for us and his amazing capacity to answer prayer along the journey of our lives. There is something here that will enlarge and challenge the understanding of both the long term believer and the one tentatively looking for answers. As you read may you be encouraged and enlarged in your vision of God; who He is and what He can do!

Yes, I must come clean. I am biased. Tanya is my daughter. I am now a retired clergyman.

There are good things here to inspire and challenge us all, even me !

Rev. David Kendrew

Former Retired Vicar of St Barnabas, Derby
and Retired Rector of St Leonard's, Deal

INTRODUCTION
"God can do infinitely more than we ever dare ask or imagine"

Do you know, God can do immeasurably and infinitely more than we would ever dare to ask or imagine?   I don't know about you, but for me, that's a huge promise that God promises to do! God is a God of surprises and He can do what seems impossible!

Each chapter in this book are amazing testimonies of God's kindness, grace and favour and of His goodness and love. He has surprised us and blessed us over and over again, in so many different ways, showing us that He is real. As I stand back and think about all God has done, I stand in awe and give Him all the honour and praise. I know and believe that everything He has done for us, He can do for your too and so very much more!

So why does He do this? Because He loves and adores us ALL!   Did you know that He loves and adores YOU! He sees and says you are amazing, special and unique! You are wonderful and precious in His eyes. He loves you with an overflowing, never ending love and this will never change or stop. His very nature and character is love. He is a loving Heavenly Father who loves you extravagantly, loves to bless you and longs to do so much more than you ever dare to ask or imagine!

Every miracle God does, points to someone who is so amazing and He is expressing His love for you.

So why this book? I am an ordinary housewife that loves Jesus and believes in God. I have seen my Heavenly Father do amazing things and have experienced His love and favour. I have experienced Him answer the 'every day' prayers like praying for parking spaces, and helping me with day to day activities as a mother, wife and homemaker. And I have also experienced and seen God do so much more, healing people, guiding and inspiring people in their lives. Opening opportunities that would not normally be possible. Speaking to people in many different ways including through pictures in my mind and dreams.

Just as I know He is real, and know Him as my Heavenly Father, I too long for all to see and know Him. To truly know that God IS interested in our 'day to day lives' and way beyond; And when we pray to Him, He can, and does do the impossible! He can and is easily able to do so much more than we ever dream, or imagine, is possible.

The Bible tells us this is how Paul knew and experienced God. He wrote a prayer that we too would experience and know that God can do superabundantly more.

'Now to Him who is able to [carry our His purpose and] do superabundantly more that all that we dare ask or think [infinitely beyond our greatest prayers, hopes or dreams], according to His power that is at work within us, to Him be the glory in the church and in Christ Jesus throughout all generations forever and ever. Amen' Ephesians 3:20 AMP

I wonder how BIG your hopes and dreams are? I invite you if you have a Bible to look up this verse and read the whole of Paul's prayer in Ephesians 3:14-21 (or check it out on The Bible App); And ask God, for an even bigger understanding of His incredible greatness and overflowing love for you! Because of Him, miracles can and do happen every day! He can do what seems impossible and every miracle points to our Heavenly Father.

As you are reading this introduction, I wonder where you are in your journey of knowing Jesus? Whether you know Him as a close friend and Saviour? Or maybe you are on a journey of exploring who Jesus is. I pray that these stories will encourage and inspire you to seek God out for yourself and know He loves you and that He is so good. He longs for you to know and experience the extensive and unending breath, width, height and length of His love. It is so huge, above and beyond, anything you have ever experienced before!

For those who believe in God, I pray that you will be inspired to trust and know with ever greater certainty, that God is for you and that He is able to do immeasurably and infinitely more than we can ever ask or imagine! That this book goes beyond a book of stories about what God has done and inspires you to know in ever increasing ways, that there is nothing that is too difficult for our Heavenly Father to do!

God can...
do infinitely more than we ask or imagine

I wonder if you have ever prayed? I wonder what sort of prayers you have prayed? For me, prayer is part of my everyday life, it is something I literally do anywhere and anytime. Prayer is like a conversation, we can talk or chat to God like a friend that we trust implicitly and He too loves to talk to us. Our Heavenly Father loves to listen to us, guide us, inspire and encourage us.

So how do we do this? We can talk to our Heavenly Father anytime, anywhere, about anything and everything. Just as you talk to a friend and spend time with them, we can do the same with our Heavenly Father. As you listen and chat to a friend and catch their perspective, you too can chat and listen to what He is saying to you by asking Him to help you catch and hear what He is saying.

If I am presented with new things or situations that I don't know what to do or how to pray I often say, 'Heavenly Father, I don't know how to pray about this. How do you want me to pray? What is your heart for this situation?'

When I pray in this way, I always find He lovingly shows me what to do. Sometimes He gives me a word, or a picture of how to pray. Often He shows me a promise that He has already given us in the Bible, which is perfect for the situation.

I have found that when I pray in this way it is like the prayer goes to a sweet spot. If you have never tried this I would encourage you to check out His promises for you, the list is endless. He has literally thought of everything!

This is a tiny glimpse of some of His promises for you…

- *He has amazing plans for you with a hope, and a future (Jeremiah 29:11 AMP)*

' "For I know the plans and thoughts that I have for you," says the Lord, "plans for peace and well-being and not for disaster, to give you a future and a hope"'
Jeremiah 29:11 Amplified Bible (AMP)

- *He will fill you with abundant joy and peace, and you will abound in hope, and overflow with confidence, in His promises for you (Romans 15:13 AMP)*

'May the God of hope fill you with all joy and peace in believing [through the experience of your faith] that by the power of the Holy Spirit you will abound in hope and overflow with confidence in His promises.'
Romans 15:13 Amplified Bible (AMP)

- *He will guide you (John 16:13, Psalm 23, Psalm 37:5, Psalm 37:23-24, Psalm 121:1-8, Psalm 119:105)*

- *He has showered you with His kindness, all wisdom and understanding [with practical insight] (Ephesians 1:8 AMP)*

- *His goodness, mercy and unfailing love will pursue you all the days of your life (Psalm 23:6b AMP)*

- *Jesus was wounded and crushed for our sins, He was beaten that we might have peace. He was whipped and we were healed (Isaiah 53:5 NLT)*

God's promises & the power of praying 'In the Name of Jesus'

The Bible is inspired by God. When we pray His promises we are saying and praying 'God's words' and promises into being. This means we can be really confident in praying these prayers, because He has already told us this is what He has promised for us.

So how did Jesus pray? One of the prayers that you may have heard or even said is the 'Lord's Prayer'. This can be found in Luke 10:1-4 and was a prayer that Jesus used to teach us to pray.

Then later in John's Gospel, Jesus was talking to His disciples saying that when they pray to pray 'In the Name of Jesus'. You may have heard those words before. When we pray and seal our prayers 'In the Name of Jesus', it is a Royal seal. This means we are praying God's promises from the Bible, 'In the Name of Jesus', believing and expecting to see our prayers answered, it carries power and authority. We are sealing and signing the prayers in the Name of the King of all kings.

This is how Jesus encouraged his disciples to pray and we too are also encouraged to do this too. Jesus said we should ask and pray 'In the Name of Jesus', because when we pray and ask in faith, like Jesus did, things happen and it gives

God glory. When Jesus was on the earth He healed the sick, enabled blind people to see, fed 5000 people with a boys packed lunch and so much more. Even these stories today seem rather amazing....but the truth is, this is the life God has for us now too! Because Jesus said,

"The truth is, anyone who believes in me
will do the same works I have done, and even greater
works, because I am going to be with the Father.
You can ask for anything in my name, and I will do it,
because the work of the Son brings glory to the Father.
Yes, ask anything in my name, and I will do it"
John 14:12-14 NLT

This is an amazing promise in our ordinary everyday lives, God can and does do extra-ordinary things. Our Heavenly Father longs for and wants you to believe and know He is for you and He loves and adores you; And He is able to answer our prayers. He wants us to come confidently to the Throne of Grace and present our prayers and thanks to Him.

As you read this book, I pray you will be inspired to pray

and believe God can do this and even greater things in your life too. He really can do over and above, superabundantly more, than we can imagine!

"I pray that you will begin to understand
the incredible greatness of His power for us who
believe him.

This is the same mighty power
that raised Christ from the dead
and seated him in the place of honour at God's right
hand in the heavenly realms.

Now He is far above any ruler or authority
or power
or leader
or anything else in this world
or in the world to come"

Ephesians 1:19-21 NLT

Miracles show us that God is here

Miracles are God's way of showing us He is here!

Chapter 1
Your Prayers are like a fragrance
God can do the impossible!

'And we can be confident that

He will listen to us whenever we ask Him for anything in line with His will. And if we know He is listening when we make our requests, we can be sure that He will give us what we ask for'

1 John 5:14-15 NLT

Can I invite you to close your eyes for one moment, and think about your favourite fragrance? What is it? What does it remind you of? And why is it so special and so beautiful?

I wonder what fragrance you thought of and what it reminds you of and why?

The reason I have asked you these questions is because, just as you have imagined a fragrance you love, God also has a favourite fragrance He loves too. Your Prayers, are like a beautiful fragrance to Him! The Bible describes our prayers as incense, which are placed in gold bowls in heaven

I find this such a beautiful way of imagining what prayer is like. Can you imagine every prayer you have prayed, or will ever pray, are precious to God, and to Him they are the most amazing fragrance. Your prayers are valued, precious and treasured and are placed in gold bowls in heaven. It's significant that the Bible says our prayers are placed in special bowls made of gold, because Gold is a precious, expensive, special and beautiful metal, valuable and of high worth. It is a picture to remind us of the value and how precious, our prayers are to God.

When I think about it, it makes me think…. WOW! Someone treasures the prayers that are spoken, or whispered, or said in my imagination. Over the years so many people all over the world have prayed prayers, including everyday people, celebrities, prime ministers, presidents, kings and queens. I wonder how gigantic those bowls must be, they must be HUGE! I wonder what the gold bowls are like, how they glisten, and shine?

I wonder how many prayers we have prayed, have resulted in further prayers being prayed and answered. As we see one answer to prayer, further opportunities often open up; And then further prayers are prayed, often without realising that the first prayer we had prayed has been so significant. This is because it has opened up far more opportunities than you would ever have realised possible, or thought of at the time!

This can be illustrated when you think of an acorn (or even a mustard seed).

Imagine an acorn in your hand (or even a Mustard seed if you have never seen an acorn!). The acorn or seed is small and seems tiny but if planted in good soil and given the right conditions it will grow to an enormous tree. In a similar way when we pray, believe and receive in faith the answers to our prayers, it is like an Oak tree growing from the tiny acorn 'prayers' we have prayed.

Every year an Oak tree will yield many thousands of acorns resulting in further opportunities for more Oak trees to grow. Similarly one prayer often leads to another answered prayer, which creates another opportunity to pray.

In a similar way, the prayers that were prayed in this first chapter, opened up many other opportunities to see God answer many other prayers. Many of the opportunities would not have happened, if that first prayer had never of been prayed!

Interestingly an Oak tree doesn't only produces acorns, but also provides food and shelter for many forms of life too. In a similar way the fruits of our prayers are encouragement for others to believe that God can and is easily able to answer our prayers. To inspire them to know, with ever increasing certainty that they too can pray, believe and know that God, can do the impossible. I pray that as you read this chapter you will be inspired to pray and see the harvest of everything God has for you.

To give a little back ground, in my twenties I was planning my birthday and decided that I would celebrate by doing something a little different with my friends. Not far from where we lived there is a Water-sports centre which has a variety of outdoor water pursuits including a Wild White Water rafting slalom course. It was going to be fun and was also to be a much bigger adventure than I had ever anticipated!

Little did I know a couple of days later I would be rushed into Hospital. Initially they suspected appendicitis. After various tests they discovered the severe pain was in actual fact a ginormous ovarian cyst. The Gynaecological Consultant, who specialised in this area for years was speechless, as he had never ever seen anything quite so big. It was the size of a full term baby!

The medical staff were amazed as I had had no symptoms or pain before being rushed into hospital; And were even more surprised that I had been white water rafting a couple of days before and the enormous cyst hadn't burst, as it would have been fatal. It was nothing short of a miracle, as it contained toxic liquid and in my case a rather lot of it!

God had protected me and kept me safe, because He had a much bigger plan.

Before operating the Consultant explained the procedure, saying there would be a strong chance that I would not be able to have children. There could be complications and ultimately I would have a very large scar. Naively I asked if he could do keyhole surgery, but was told it was totally out of the question as the cyst was so huge and they were concerned it might be cancerous.

As a Christian, I wasn't worried by the words, but had a peace knowing that God was with me and miracles were possible. I prayed along with my family and friends, that the operation would be successful and that actually, God would enable me to have children in the future.

The operation went well. The cyst and all the toxic contents were successfully removed and the incision was tiny and so much smaller than they expected. In fact it was so small that nobody would be aware I had even had major surgery, apart from the fact I had to take things very easy for several weeks. The cyst was benign but, the Consultant again advised that I would now have a very slim or no chance of having children. And if I was lucky enough, I would only have a very small window of 2 to 3 years maximum.

Unshaken by this news, I knew in my heart that if I was meant to have children God would and could enable it to happen.

Several years later I met and married my amazing husband Tony, who knew of the situation, but we had complete peace, and a sense that God would bless us with a child when the time was right. Eight years after the operation we decided that we would love to start a family.

I wonder if you have ever prayed? As a Christian I know I can confidently pray to my Heavenly Father. I often pray by myself, anytime, anywhere and about anything. Sometimes it's a quick prayer and other times I take space to pray and spend time with God.

There is also something special about praying with another Christian, or Christians as there is added weight to our prayers when we pray together in agreement. This time, I knew that it would be good to pray with someone.

So I spoke to Dawn and we prayed together that God would bless us with a child. Thanking God for His promise that we could be confident that He will listen (1 John 5:14-15).

'And we can be confident that He will listen to us whenever we ask Him for anything in line with His will. And if we know He is listening when we make our requests, we can be sure that He will give us what we ask for' 1 John 5:14-15 NLT

And thanking Him for His promise, that when He created the world He blessed all that He had made and told it to multiply and fill the earth (Genesis 1:28 NLT).

Amazingly, completely against the odds, within 2 months God answered our prayers. I was pregnant naturally over 8 years after the operation! It was a miracle, a "created miracle", God had done what seemed impossible!

Also at the same time as I was praying I would become pregnant, I also secretly prayed and asked God that we might have a little girl. I didn't tell anyone about this, as I didn't know whether this could really happen and even if, God could answer such a specific prayer.

Throughout the pregnancy God was with us, and I was given a brilliant book called 'Praying for your Unborn Child'[1] by Francis and Judith Macnutt which spoke about the different stages in a baby's development and gave ideas of how to pray for our baby. Inspired by this book and other things I had read, we prayed for our baby, that he or she would have a safe and normal delivery and that God would pour out His blessings and love upon our baby.

A few months into the pregnancy we had a scare, the prognosis wasn't good and we were told I might miss-carry. Again we prayed and our family, and our church family at St Nic's Nottingham prayed that God would sustain and protect it, knowing that God promised this child would be fearfully and wonderfully made and He already knew it (Psalm 139:13-16 AMP). Everything then settled down and the rest of my pregnancy went like a dream.

To our delight, our baby was born with no complications or problems. And there was another miracle, not only did we have a baby when we were told it would be impossible,

---

[1] F. MacNutt & J. MacNutt, Praying for your unborn child (London: Great Britian, 2002)

For more information see www.christianhealingmin.org

31

but God had heard my 'secret prayers' and we had the most beautiful gift of a daughter!! It was a 'double miracle'!

God has continued to answer our prayers as she is the happiest and most joyful, daughter. And He has poured out His blessings upon her in so many different ways!

Even at a very young age she has seen God work in her life and she too, has an amazing faith in Jesus. For us she is one of the few treasures who I believe will be with us in Heaven, because she knows Jesus as her personal friend.

Little did I realise when we prayed those prayers many years before that, God would bless us with the miracle of a daughter. These life changing prayers helped me to realise, expect and know, in my heart, that God cares about 'every detail' of our lives. He loves us all and He is able to perform miracles and every time He does, it's His way of showing us that with God all things are possible.

I believe God encourages us to believe and pray, not just through a single lens, with wishful thinking; but He longs for us to see the **'Bigness and Greatness'** of who He is and the endless possibilities we have in Him. He longs for you to share your life and each day with Him and experience all that God has for us.

God is so much closer than you think. You can talk to Him like you would a friend. You don't need special words or a special voice. You can talk to Him about anything and everything.

Have you ever prayed or talked to God? If you prayed a prayer now, what would you pray?

Your Prayers are a beautiful fragrance to your Heavenly Father and they are placed in precious, glistening, gold bowls in Heaven. They are treasured and precious and He loves to answer them!

Miracles are God's way of showing us He is here!

Chapter 2
GOD SPEAKS TO CHILDREN
Signs and wonders – a pattern of a dress

Jesus said "'When the Spirit of Truth comes, he will guide you into all truth. He will not be presenting his own ideas; he will be telling you what he has heard. He will tell you about the future. He will bring me glory by revealing to you whatever he receives from me'" John 16: 13-14 (NLT)

God speaks to everyone and there is no age barrier! He can guide us and inspire us in day to day lives. And He helps us to understand and to know Him, His personality, His character and how lavishly He loves us.

Often people think that God will speak to us just when we are doing things such as reading the Bible, praying, or when we worship Him. However, we can talk to God and hear Him speak to us not only at church, but at home, work, school, in the car, really anywhere and at any time. He is a Heavenly Father who loves to talk to us.

He speaks in many different ways. He speaks to us through the Holy Spirit in the most amazing and incredible ways. It may not be an audible voice (although sometimes it is), but He speaks in many different ways and often uses our senses. So, it might be something we hear, see, taste, touch, feel or smell.

For example, it may be a word or words spoken that resonate, or music you listen to. Perhaps something that you are inspired by which you see in a natural sense. It may be a thought that comes to mind, that makes your heart go 'wow', like a light bulb moment.

Everywhere we turn, we can sense someone is trying to talk to us. At other times you may be wondering if God is speaking to you. The answer is Yes, He always is!

Often the best way to talk with God, is to find a place and create space to just take a moment, to be still and listen. You could tell Him about your day, what's on your mind; And then ask Him what's on His mind and what He wants to tell you. Even in the busyness and the hustle and bustle of our lives God can speak, it just takes a moment for us to catch what He is saying.

Whenever He speaks, or whatever He reveals to us, it's always in a loving way because that's the very nature and character of God. You will always have a real sense of complete peace, or excitement knowing what you've just received is perfect for that situation. And it's always surrounded and covered in His perfect, abundant love.

The reason for this is that He knows and understands us perfectly. He loves us all and always speaks in a way we can understand, whatever our age or ability. There is no one too young or too old.

This next chapter, is an example of how God speaks in a way we can understand and is a lovely illustration of how God spoke to our daughter, who was just 6 years old at the time. Revealing a pattern to her, which resulted in the most amazing opportunity for her to flourish and excel. It was life changing!

Our daughter Grace, was in Year 2 at primary school. Every Sunday we would travel to church in the car. I would often lead, or help, in the children's Sunday school sessions, along with other volunteers. Over the previous months we had been chatting with the children about how we can pray to our Heavenly Father and can chat to Him about anything. And He also loves to listen to us and chat to us too.

If you want to read more about this there are lots of great books on this subject.

One Sunday morning as we were travelling back home from church our daughter said "Mummy, a picture has come into my head". She then explained "I think God has given me a picture of dots and squares". I asked her what the colours of the dots and squares were and she then replied "There are red dots and blue squares. What do you think this might mean?"

Not knowing what this meant, I said I wasn't quite sure and maybe she could chat and pray to God and ask Him. Then a few minutes later, she said "Mummy, God has made the dots and squares into star shapes and a star shaped pattern! What do you think it might mean?". Still not sure what this unusual picture was, I suggested she drew the pattern onto a piece of paper and maybe we should pray together in the car.

Knowing there must be an explanation for this unusual picture, we prayed and asked God to show us and what He was trying to say to us. As the Bible promises, in John 16:13, that the Holy Spirit will guide us.

As we continued to drive home, we prayed and thanked God for the picture. Thanking Him, that He promises to help us understand what He is saying to us and asking that He would reveal to us what this pattern meant.

The following day my husband and I were chatting about how excited we were that our daughter was showing an aptitude for music and sport and wondering if it might be good to explore a different school that would give her greater opportunity to excel in these areas, as her current school didn't have extensive music or sports facilities. So, I started to do some research, contacted a number of schools, checking facilities, ordering prospectuses and then made appointments with our top 3 preferred schools.

When the prospectuses arrived, we looked through the details and to my surprise one of them had intriguing pictures! As I looked at the photographs I noticed the school uniform might have been blue, red and white in colour! I wondered if there might be a link with Grace's drawing.

I made appointments to meet all the various Heads of the three schools. We discussed the facilities, looked around the schools and met some of the children.

One of the schools took us by surprise. Not only did they have an impressive academic history plus amazing sports facilities, a wide range of opportunities and extra-curricular activities to explore and try, but also (unusually) had a dedicated music school with extensive music facilities.

As we were walking around the school with the Headmaster, we had the opportunity to meet some of the children. I noticed the girls were wearing summer uniform, but to my surprise it looked different from the usual summer dresses primary schools have.

To those of you reading this book, in the UK usually in the summer term, girls at Primary school wear gingham checked summer dresses. Often these are either blue and white, or red and white, or green and white. However, as I looked more closely I noticed the girl's summer dresses had a more unusual pattern. Not a usual gingham check, but it had a red, blue and white 'star shaped' pattern!

I couldn't believe my eyes! It looked like the intricate pattern which God had given our daughter, just a week earlier (which she had drawn on a piece of white paper, with red dots and blue squares in a star shape). It was in actual fact identical to the pattern on the girl's dresses!

How could this be? It was a school we had never been to before, we didn't know anyone who went to the school and it was situated on completely different side of the

City from where we lived, some 15 miles away. How could our 6 years old daughter, ever have known a pattern like this, other than God had revealed it to her?

As we left, the Headmaster suggested if we wanted to consider the school further, that our daughter could come and visit for a day and take an entrance exam. He said there was no guarantee of a place, as the entrance test was challenging and they were always oversubscribed for places. In addition to this, they only had a limited number of places available for her academic year.

Totally lost for words and excited by all I had seen and heard, we arranged for our daughter to visit and take the entrance exam. Praying that God would make things clear and show us if this was where she should go to school. And if it was, she would be offered a place.

To our delight Grace loved her taster day and was offered a place to start just a few months later in the Autumn Term in September. We had so much peace and were so thrilled and excited because we knew this was exactly where Grace should be. As we thought about our journey to explore a new school we were lost for words in awe and wonder at how God had given our daughter a perfect picture of the intricate patten of her summer dress of the new school. It was a 'sign', and nothing short of a miracle!

As her first day approached we organised the new school uniform. In the UK, often children start in the Autumn Term (September), in their winter uniforms and only wear their summer uniforms in the Summer Term from around Easter to the end of the summer term. However, to our surprise, we discovered the girls start back in September in their summer uniforms, for Grace this meant she was going to be wearing her new white summer cotton dress (with the intricate pattern with red dots and blue squares which formed stars), which God had shown her! How did God know that Grace would be wearing it on her first day at school!?!?

Then as time went by, as I washed and ironed the uniform, I looked more closely at the fine detail of the pattern. Not only do the red dots and blue dots form stars, but when you look closely at the fine outline of the red dot, it is edged in a star outline too! Just like our daughter had seen in the picture God had given her. It is so amazing!

Within 3 months of being at this school, Grace's confidence soared and she blossomed even more academically and musically. It was and still is the perfect place, where every child is celebrated and encouraged. God knew our daughter, He had a perfect plan for her, which He already knew in advance. It was a much bigger and more beautiful plan than we could have imagined, somewhere where she would be encouraged, nurtured and grow in confidence, ability and in her gifts and talents.

I find it so beautiful that God chose to lovingly reveal something to our daughter first, so she was part of this amazing journey and seeing that God has such a special plan for her life.   It's incredible to think God knew how to reveal the patten to her gradually, so that she knew in detail the shapes and pattern and nothing could be lost, or mistaken. Showing her something that was totally unique, that she would never have seen, or known before. And this intricate detail would form part of the uniform she would be wearing on her first day in her new school! This will always be a significant memory, for Grace to treasure, because it was something that God revealed and showed to her. Even from an early age she knows that God has and always will guide her, by His Holy Spirit.

Just as God guided us, He can do it for you too. This story is a miracle, a sign, that causes us to know God can and does speak to us, whatever our age, ability or understanding. He reveals the most amazing, beautiful and perfect things. All we have to do is ask Him to make Himself known to us and guide us. He will always reply, because He promises He will.

Is there something that you would like to ask God?

Why don't you take a moment to chat to Him. And then, take a moment to listen to what He says to you. He is your Heavenly Father, and He delights in hearing your voice and answering your prayers.

Miracles are God's way of showing us He is here!

Chapter 3
AWESOME PLANS
How God guides and leads us

"'I know the plans I have for you' says the LORD.
'They are plans for good and not disaster, to give you a future
and a hope'"
Jeremiah 29:11 NLT.

God has amazing plans for our lives and they are always good! Part of that plan is that He longs for us all to know Him as our Heavenly Father. Someone we can have a really close and special friendship with. And also, for us to journey with Him, to see and experience the fullness of everything that He has for us.

Let's just take a moment and think about someone who is special to you that you love, or you know. This might be a father, mother, spouse, brother or sister or friend. I wonder how much you love them, and how much they love you? How do you express your love to them? How do they demonstrate love to you?

Maybe you have heard them say the words to you 'I love you to the moon and back', or you have a favourite or treasured memory. Just in those words or moments, it is an expression of the length and breath of the love they have for you.

It's a beautiful and amazing feeling knowing and experiencing love. Knowing that you are completely loved, appreciated and adored. It is such a life changing experience. When someone loves you, they stand with you through thick and thin, they are someone who is dependable, who you can always rely on.

Did you know there is someone else who also loves you? He loves you even more than the person or people you have just thought of. Someone who loves you infinitely more than 'to the moon and back'.

He loves you more than all the grains of sand in the world, more than all the stars in the sky. He adores you, before you say a word, or you do anything He says 'I LOVE YOU!'. He has placed His hand of blessing on your head. That person is your Heavenly Father.

He sees you and knows you are so amazing. You are the apple of His eye. He longs for you to truly know and experience the love He has for you in ever increasing ways.

Jesus and the apostle Paul, had a deep understanding and revelation of God's love for them, as a Heavenly Father. In fact this was Jesus's prayer for us, that we too would know the Father's love. He wanted us to truly know and experience God's love, because He knew that God loves us as much as He loves Him (Jesus)! What an amazing thought! Your Heavenly Father wants to lavishly surround and fill you with His love. He loves you like no other person can.

Having a deep sense of love from someone impacts the way we express our love and the names and the words we use to speak, or talk to that person. Interestingly, both Jesus and Paul knew with complete certainty how deep, how wide and how broadly God loved and knew them. This is reflected in the words that they used to talk to God. They used the name 'Abba, Father' to talk to God their Heavenly Father.

'Abba' in Aramaic means 'The Father'. When Jesus said the words 'Abba Father', He was recognising and acknowledging the power of God and expressing His admiration. It was a passionate and intimate expression of someone who He knew loved Him, relentlessly and passionately.

We are all invited, whether we are young or old, man or woman, or a child we are all invited to know God as our 'Abba Father'. We can know and experience Him as our Heavenly Father. We become His children. This is what we become when we know God as our Heavenly Father and invite Jesus into our lives, as our friend and saviour. We too, are given a special and privileged status and become His sons, and daughters.

We too can know and experience this warm, personal experience with God the Father, our Heavenly Father. He knows all things. Before we even speak, or do anything, He knows our greatest strengths and weaknesses. He loves to inspire and guide us. However, He doesn't force His will on us, but lovingly allows us to meet Him, in our own personal way. Like a shepherd knows and looks after his sheep, He too loves and cares for each one of us and loves us enough to give us everything we need, and loves to answer your prayers.

This next chapter is an example of how we can know God as a Heavenly Father. Someone we can be in relationship with and loves to inspire us, guide us and lead us. Both in our everyday lives and also in 'Big' decisions we make. He does this through The Holy Spirit, whom Jesus promised would come and would be our guide, helper and encourager.

So, how does He do this? Simply, all we need to do is ask. He doesn't guide us by imposing or forcing ideas on us, but simply waits for us to ask. When He inspires and guides, it's always loving and not controlling. It is always peaceful and lines up with the what the Bible says. It always brings a sense of peace, that is perfect for the situation.

Have you ever been in a situation or had an opportunity but you didn't know what to do? Maybe you are currently pondering over decisions you have to make?

In this next chapter, I share how I have been exploring and thinking about going to theological college, to study a course focusing on Children's Ministry. I had been praying as I loved helping with the children's work at our church and I wondered if this course seemed a natural progression in order to have a greater Biblical and practical understanding of why and how we can offer opportunities for children to encounter and know God in a real way. And maybe God was leading me into this ministry in a deeper way.

As I prayed I knew God had chosen me and He invited me not to be afraid, because He had called me by name.

That what He was about to do, was nothing compared with what He had already done. He was going to lead me on a journey of trusting Him and doing something completely new.

It was a really exciting, as I had never been to university and the course was at Cliff College, and was a course approved by and leading to an award of The University of Manchester. There were blocks of teaching weeks, with practical application at our home church. However, there were also other considerations to heed if, I was offered a place, as I would also need help with child care. Our daughter was at school and sometimes my husband was away with work on business.

Wow! To my delight, everything fell into place. The Letter arrived, I was offered a place to go and also my dad offered to come and stay, and look after our daughter and take her school when I was away for study weeks. It was so significant that my dad offered to come, as it was like God had given us an opportunity to work together and it was a wonderful opportunity for him to have special time with his granddaughter. It was like a role reversal that had happened many years before, when I stayed and encouraged my dad years ago.

Little did I know the other opportunities that God was also going to open up. One of these was the research project for my dissertation.

For many years, I had seen that children have an amazing and natural disposition to express their awe and wonder at everything. Whether it was something new they had discovered, or they were shown, to them everything was so exciting and full of wonder!

But, I was puzzled too, by the fact that children so often seemed unengaged in worship, and I often wondered why? How could this be? I knew my Heavenly Father was so real, and amazing to me, and I loved to reflect this when I worshipped. But why weren't they coming enthusiastically, and joyously to worship? I knew in the Bible there were many occasions where Jesus encouraged children to come to him, because He loved them and loved to bless them. Even in the Old Testament, in Psalms it says that God taught children to praise Him (Psalm 8:2 NLT).

I wondered if God loves children and all people so much and longs for them to know Him in a real and personal way, how can we encourage and enable children to engage in worshipping God? And how can this be done in a way that is appropriate for them? How can their natural sense of exploration and their ability to express awe and wonder, be expressed in worship?

As I prayed about my research project I had a strong sense that God was calling me and inspiring me to explore this further through my dissertation. At the time, as I prayed, I had a sense this invitation would extend above and beyond a thesis and God would enable it to be used after the course had finished. It would be something much bigger than I realised. But I didn't know how.

During the teaching week where the lecturers gave us guidance about how to choose a research project, I was struck by the importance of worship and committing our ideas to God in prayer. One particular person who was leading the Course, was Ian White. He has such a passion for sharing Jesus with other people, both in the UK and all around the world. It was the core and centre of everything that he believed and did. However when he gave the lecture on worship, I was struck by the fact that even though mission and sharing Jesus was central to everything that he did, he knew worship was even more important than that. He was passionate about worshipping God!

To me, it was a massive 'light bulb' moment to see someone so passionate about worshipping and even more than the call of sharing, and telling others about Jesus. The 'penny dropped' when I realised the importance of worshipping and praising God. When we worship and praise our Heavenly Father, we are expressing our love to Him and why He is so special. When you really love someone, you really desire to express that love to them. In a similar way when we catch a glimpse of how awesome, and amazing God is and all He's done, you eagerly seek to praise Him, and thank Him!

I wonder, have you asked God to reveal himself to you? Have you ever had a moment where you have been awestruck by what He is like or by what He has done?

This 'light bulb' moment fueled even more desire to explore worship with the children and confirm that this is what God wanted me to do.

As I thought and prayed about it further, I was led to reflect on how Jesus encourages us to 'worship in spirit and in truth', when he spoke to a Samaritan Woman at the well, in John 4:23-24 (NLT). Telling her that true worshippers, worshipped in spirit and in truth. As I reflected on this I felt in a sense it was important to ask the Holy Spirit to inspire us not only as we worshipped, but also as we prepared and wrote the material; That He would inspire the children, and us as leaders to understand our Heavenly Father more and this would be reflected in our expression of worship.

This is something that you can do right now, you can ask God to help you understand and know Him as your 'Abba Father', your 'Heavenly Father'.

Initially I shared my vision and ideas, with a number of my Christian friends who were either parents, grandparents, or God parents. We formed a prayer team to pray for the children. Asking the Holy Spirit to inspire and enable us to encounter and engage with God. So, the children could know Him in a real and tangible way, as their Heavenly Father. And that He would lead and guide us, as we planned, wrote, and lead the time with the children.

A few days before the first session we shared our ideas with the children's parents, asking them to partner with us and to pray for the children. We gave every child a card, as a personal invitation to come to a special Sunday school session which we called "Ablaze Worship".

Praying together and in agreement, is such a powerful thing to do, as extra-ordinary things happen when we gather together to pray. Not only is there power or added weight when praying together in unity, but there is something very special about being part of a team. When you see God answer prayers it is so powerful and causes you to trust and believe, that if God has done something for you or someone else, He can easily do it again!

If you've never done this before I'd really encourage you to find another Christian with whom you can pray, or gather together and pray. It's so much fun and a great way to pray and encourage each other in the Christian faith.

Technology is also a great way to connect in prayer. Mobiles can be a wonderful way of being connected with people and also create an amazing opportunity to pray too. We have church groups and friendship groups that we've set up on App's such as 'WhatsApp', where you can share prayer requests and answers to prayers with trusted friends.

From the very first Ablaze Worship session, which is now many years ago, to the current date we have had the most amazing times with the children worshipping God. We have discovered our worship can be vibrant, in high definition colour, as our creativity and senses bring colour to our worship. This too is reflected in Psalms, which encourages us and says every part of us can praise God 'from our head to our toes'. It's not just using our voices and singing, although that's really important, but every part of us can praise God - our hands, our feet, our body, our imagination, our senses and our touch.

This is just how children, and young people love to engage in learning. We have often found adults love to have opportunities to express their worship in this way too.

Exploring worship with the children, and young people, has been an amazing journey of many answered prayers. Every time, before planning, preparing or leading an Ablaze Worship Session we pray, inviting the Holy Spirit to inspire and lead us. It has led to incredible results! Without fail we have always known exactly what to do.

There have been so many stories of children as young as 4 years old, young people and adults who have not only engaged in worship but love worshipping God in a multi-sensory way. It has given them the freedom to express their love and praise to God and also listen to what God is sharing with them.

Children have written songs, both individually and as a whole group. One song written by five children (who were aged only 5 years old at the time) and inspired by God was:-

I will praise You!

Verse 1
I will worship You!
You are wonderful and glorious
Because You made us
And because You are brilliant at being awesome!

Chorus:
You are glorious!
You are great!
You are amazing!
Yes, You are amazing!

Verse 2
I will praise You
You are the best of them all
Because You are at the heart of my life
And Your love will never break

In another service, there was some play doh, and various creative items available; a boy prayed and listened to God and the Holy Spirit inspired him and gave him a picture of what God's love is like. The boy then took some play doh and created two hearts, which he intertwined. He explained that one heart represented God, and the other was him, and that he knew God loved him and he was expressing his love for God, and this was why the hearts were intertwined.

As the little boy listened and chatted to God further, he then created a play doh car and explained that God was like a car, that was able to move around and that anyone can sit in the car and know Him as a Heavenly Father.

I wonder if you ever realised God is with you now? He is waiting for your invitation.

Young people too, have loved writing their own love songs to Jesus and adapting other well-known songs too. On one occasion as we prayed and planned for Sunday School, we were led to focus on our Heavenly Father being our Guardian, and we used Psalm 121(MSG).

We set up three different multi-sensory spaces to worship, one of those was a singing place, where the children had opportunity to express their own song of worship to God. Worship is a personal response to express our love and this song reflects their expression of love, using their understanding and words.

My Guardian, based on Psalm 121

Chorus:
With me in the good times,
With me in the bad times
I'm not going to worry
You 're always with me
You shine on me, God
And you Keep shining
You're always by me,
My Guardian

Verse:
Better than Marshmallows
My Guardian
You shine like stars of all the Heavens
of His creation
You take care of me
you can help me through
Every step I take, be there forever
for all eternity

In another Ablaze Worship session children aged 4-6 years old, created their own song based on one of the Psalms. This has been put to music and is sung in church.

God has answered our prayers. Every time without fail He shows us what to do and how to do it. Material has been used in different churches, different settings, by children, young people and people of all ages. He has opened up opportunities for the material to be further developed and used for specific age groups, so the material is bespoke for ages, abilities and different settings.

When we take a moment and ask God to inspire us and guide us, the most amazing things happen. It is like a deer being taken to 'mountain top places'. Exploring and seeing things from at higher perspective, from God's perspective.

I believe God knows us personally as individuals and speaks in ways we can understand and we can know it is His loving voice talking to us too. He longs for us to encounter Him in a real and tangible way. Journeying with us through our lives, being an encourager, inspirer, innovator, creator God leading us on amazing adventures with Him.

I stand in awe of all that has happened, from a simple prayer asking God about whether I should go to Theological college and what the focus of my research project should be; And how we should approach it, what we should do, how the material should be written and shared. Then seeing the fruit of those prayers answered as we've seen people of different ages and backgrounds engaging in worship and growing in their understanding of who God is to them; also them experiencing and knowing a close friendship with their Heavenly Father. Some for the first time and others growing in their friendship with Him.

There is an invitation for you too.

He has amazing plans for your life. He longs for you and all of us to experience the fullness of life in every way. When we take up His invitation, He takes us to 'high places', similar to the picture at the beginning of the chapter. God gives greater perspective, from higher ground, to see the fullness of everything He has for us to step into.

Are there things you have on you mind that you would love to know how to approach well? Have you decisions to make or opportunities to explore, that you would welcome someone to guide you through?

There is someone you can talk to, and that person is Jesus.

Miracles are God's way of showing us He is here!

Chapter 4
BLESSINGS AND SURPRISES
Superabundantly more than you can imagine!

"Now to Him who is able to [carry out His purpose and] do superabundantly more than all that we dare ask or think [infinitely beyond our greatest prayers, hopes or dreams], according to His power that is at work within us, to Him be the glory in the church and in Christ Jesus throughout all generations forever and ever. Amen." Ephesians 3:20–21 (AMP)

I believe and know that God loves to surprise and bless us and it's often in ways we never expect!

I meet regularly with a close friend to catch up and pray. Over the years our prayers have been about many different things. We have seen God answer so many prayers, from prayers for our families that our children have perfect teachers at school, favour with passports and visas, friends to be healed, freedom from allergies and overwhelming peace in challenging situations. The list is endless!

God always blesses us and surprises us, and that's what He can do for you. I believe God loves to answer our 'Big prayers' and He doesn't need to be reserved for those big, seemingly difficult times, but He loves to partner with us in our everyday lives and in every part of our lives.

One of my everyday prayers can be something so simple, like praying for a parking space. This was something that someone suggested many years ago when I wasn't sure if God really answered prayers. For some people to immediately pray and believe God can do a miracle, might seem a wonderful idea and one they've heard of in Sunday school classes or R.E. lessons as a child, or in church. To see it and experience it, is a totally different thing. However, when you experience, see and know God can answer prayers, it builds faith to trust and believe, that if God has done it once, He can do it again and dare to believe God can do so much more.

That's exactly what Ephesians 3:20-21 is saying, at the beginning of this chapter. Our Heavenly Father longs for and wants to do, so much more than we ever dare ask or think is possible. He can do what seems impossible and make it possible!

It's a bit like riding a bike, once you have peddled and practised you become more proficient and you can then ride a bike with confidence because you know that you can balance on two wheels. You can trust the bike to hold your weight and as you pedal, you will be able to ride a bike. It is something that you can do naturally and becomes an everyday thing you believe and you know you can do.

In a similar way, God wants us to know and believe He is for us and loves us and He loves to answer our prayers. He wants us to come confidently into the Throne Room of His Grace and present our prayers and thanks to Him.

One of the keys to understanding prayer, is to know that God always *listens and replies* to our prayers. Sometimes we might think that He hasn't answered our prayers, but actually He has, in a different way to what we were expecting because He has a more perfect plan. Other times all we need to do is to ask Him to help us recognise His voice, and take a moment to listen and catch what He is saying to us. The way He **answers** our prayers varies, He only wants to give us good things that are right and perfect for us, because He is our Heavenly Father.

So how do you know what you can pray and what prayers God will answer? By reading the Bible, you will find so many promises that are waiting for you to discover. Those promises are as relevant today as they were yesterday, or in years gone by. He promises to guide us, inspire us, heal us, comfort us, to be with us, to give us His perfect peace and His abundant overflowing joy are just some of the promises He loves to fulfil.

As I grew in my understanding that God loves to answer our prayers I had a 'light bulb' moment of discovery, when I realised the power and importance of praying 'In the Name of Jesus'. When we pray in this way, it's like a

Royal Seal for our prayers and enables our prayers to be prayed using Jesus's authority, and literally in His name.

Jesus spoke about this in John 14:1-14, where He promised that when we believe in Jesus we can pray prayers 'In the Name of Jesus'. We will do the same things that He did and greater, because when these prayers are answered, it shows how amazing He is, and literally glorifies God.

When you consider all the things Jesus did in his short ministry here on earth, it is really amazing. Imagine reading a C.V. which described someone who turned water into wine, fed five thousand people with five loaves and two fishes, made the blind to see, deaf to hear, lame to walk, brought the dead to life. Wouldn't that make you wonder and ask yourself who this man is? Why would He do this and how did He do this?

For Jesus to even suggest to us that we will do the same as Him is incredible, but to know and believe, we can do, is amazing!

Jesus is the same as all those years ago, as He is today and forever. He wants us to believe we too can pray the prayers He prayed and people can be healed and set free.

Miracles, signs and wonders can and do happen every day when we pray 'In the Name of Jesus'.

In our church there are members of our congregation who have seen people who were once blind or partially sighted, but can now see, because Jesus has healed them. People who have had heart conditions and who are now completely healed, having these conditions verified both before and after by the medical profession. People who could not move joints in their body due to having surgical pins, or having certain conditions, are now able to move their feet and legs into positions they could never do before!

I too, was healed of thyroid problems. My medical records and blood tests have shown for several years that my thyroid was border line, requiring medication for life, due to an under active thyroid but now I no longer have any problems with my thyroid because Jesus has healed me. I also previously had an allergy to chocolate and had suffered from Hay fever but now I no longer have any symptoms. Our Heavenly Father can answer our everyday prayers, which might seem small and insignificant but He is able to answer our big bold prayers too.

Why don't you take a moment to think about the verse at the beginning of the chapter from Ephesians, I wonder what your 'highest prayers, hopes and dreams are'?

This next chapter are stories from a holiday to the States, which ring out how God answers so many prayers, in practical ways and often blesses us in ways that we don't expect. To set the scene, we were planning a family vacation to The States. It was a road trip starting in the centre of Washington, then a few nights by the coast and finishing in New York. As we planned our itinerary we each chose one thing we'd love to do whilst we were away. My husband loves to play golf and was keen to play at either of one of two prestigious Golf Courses which were not far from where we were staying. Our daughter was really keen to visit a particular toy store, that is only in America and I said I would love to go to a service at a Hillsong church New York. Arranging to go to a toy store and church are easy to organise, however the Golf was a little more tricky The course my husband really wanted to play on was one of the Top 100 Golf Courses in the world and was a members only club. He wasn't a member of the club, and didn't know any members.

Little did we know that as we prayed, God would open up the 'perfect door' for us and not only this, He would do so much more than what we ever expected or asked for!

Before we flew out to the States, my husband had been in touch with various people to see if they had any contacts to arrange a round of golf at one of the prestigious golf courses, only to discover they too were unsuccessful.

So, my prayer partner, Sarah and I, decided to pray and ask for God's favour, that somehow God would open an opportunity for my husband to play golf. Just before we left to go on holiday, the Golf Club got in touch and confirmed to my husband that even though it was a members only Club he would be able to play a round of golf. At that point they couldn't say which course, as they were having work done on the greens. Again, we prayed the work would go well on the golf course and the grass would recover in time so that he would be able to play on the prestigious East Course. To our delight a couple of days before he was due to play, they said the work on the golf course was going well and he would in actual fact be able to play a round of golf on their prestigious 'East course', with the Assistant Pro! His friends could not believe what had happened, he was going to play where a number of Golf Championships have been held!

Another time on the trip, when we prayed, God opened doors for us on one of the days we were staying in Washington. We planned to visit The Capitol Building & Congress and were standing in the queue to book tickets to take a Tour exploring the Capital Building & Congress, only to discover if we wanted to see The House of Representatives we needed both our passport and also a letter of commendation by a Senate, enabling us to visit these areas. Neither of which we had with us.

To add to this, as we waited and queued there was a security alert announced in the building. This resulted in a number of the Tours being cancelled and those that were available, were now fully booked. No time scale was given as to when the security alert would be lifted and the staff were recommending everyone to either come back another day, or those that wanted to stay could book tickets to watch a film about the history of Capitol Building in the theatre and then explore the museum.

Not put off by this, we prayed that the security issue would be resolved and somehow we might be able to see more of the exhibits in the Capitol Building & Congress. Believing that God could do what seemed impossible and trusting that somehow He would make it happen. Knowing miracles can happen when we pray and trust God!

As we waited, we watched the film and explored the museum. Whilst we were in the museum I noticed a museum curator and asked him if he could explain how Congress and the House of Representatives compared to the Parliamentary system in the UK.

As he was explaining it to me he asked if we'd ever been to the Capital Building before and seen the State rooms, to which I replied no. I explained unfortunately we had missed out on tickets to The State Rooms, which I understood were limited as a result of the security alert.

Totally out of the blue he asked me who I was travelling with, placed his hand in his jacket pocket and pulled out three special passes to see inside The House of Representatives. We were totally speechless, as these passes were usually given out by Senators, and these tickets gave us access to not only

The House of Representatives, but to the Congress and rest of the Capital Building. Somehow God had answered our prayer! We were going to be able to look around the whole of the building!

The next stage of our trip involved travelling on a train. We were travelling from Philadelphia to New York. Our primary concern was that our train didn't have a designated luggage carriage and we had noticed that there might be restrictions with dimensions of bags, which would mean we might have a problem with three international suitcases, a full set of golf clubs, not to mention hand luggage.

However, unworried by this, we knew we could pray because the Bible says in Philippians 4:19 (NLT), that God takes care of us and will supply all our needs. Before leaving our hotel, my daughter and I prayed that somehow God would help us in the next part of our journey and He would enable us to sit with our luggage. That there would be no problem with the size or quantity of luggage and that all the travel connections would fit perfectly together, so that we would be able to go to Hillsong Church New York that evening.

When we arrived at the station we noticed that passengers were gathering in the main station and then once checked in, were allowed to go down a steep escalator to board the train. This in theory was fine, but we had rather a large amount of bulky luggage to negotiate on the rather narrow and step escalators!

From nowhere a man wearing uniform appeared with a big trolley and approached us saying, "You have a lot of luggage would you like some assistance? I can take you somewhere where you will have lots of space and all your luggage with you on the train. You will be able to get onto the train now, before everyone else!" Slightly surprised by this kind invitation, we took a second look at the man, noticing he was wearing uniform and had an identity badge and decided to place our luggage onto the trolley and follow him. He brought us to a big wide open carriage, with the most enormous free space, where we could not only place all of our luggage but there were four seats that were right next to it as well! Wow!

As we looked up to thank the man, he said to us "The train is full, and this carriage will fill up completely, but you will be fine here". I then looked at the man's identity badge, and realized it said 'Angel'!

Wow, how did God do that! He had not only answered our prayer in helping us to get on the train with all our enormous array of luggage, but He had also sent a man to help us, called Angel or maybe it was God's way of telling us He had sent an angel to help us? It was abundantly clear God not only cared for us, but He provided us with all the help we needed! Just like He promises in Philippians 4:19.

Each morning whilst we were in New York, we prayed that God would bless and guide us and that we would be a blessing and encouragement to others too whilst we were away.

One of these mornings before we left, I felt prompted by the Holy Spirit to place a small book about prayer called 'There is Hope[2]' in my bag. As we were having breakfast I received a message from the worship team at our church back home, encouraging us to write a song of praise, but saying it shouldn't be an ordinary song but 'Heaven's song', a song that God inspires the words and leads us to sing.

---

[2] For more information about the booklet or to get a copy of 'There is Hope' can be found on www.trypraying.org

As I sat and chatted, and listened to God, the Holy Spirit inspired me to write a song which I wrote onto my phone. I felt a sense that the words He had given me were a song to sing for those we would see and meet later that day and were a song for the city of New York. Little did I know that God was going to use this song later that morning!

As we went about our day we decided that we would explore if it might be possible to organise tickets for a show on Broadway. As we went up out of the escalator at Times Square, we were looking for a ticket office where we could organise last minute tickets on Broadway. Not knowing where to go, I saw a police lady and I also knew she was the person God wanted me to speak to.

We asked her for directions and then by surprise she shared that she was a Christian and God had placed a song on her heart that morning which she had been singing as a prayer for the City of New York, by a world-renowned gospel singer songwriter. As she shared the song words, I was speechless as the song God had given her that morning was a song asking for God to come into our world. And it echoed the one He had inspired me to write just a few hours earlier!

Lord will you walk into this place
Pour out Your Spirit we pray
Fill this place with Your presence, Lord
We need You today

For You are our strength
You are our peace
Fill every corner and every crevice
So every part is alight with Your presence

We love to be in the Shadow of the Lord Almighty
For You are good
You are kind
In Your presence is peace and fullness of joy!
For You are good
You are kind
In Your presence is peace and fullness of joy!

As we continued to chat she said she had been asking God to show her new ways to pray and immediately I knew this was the person God wanted me to give the little book to! Within the book it had ideas of how to pray creatively. It's a brilliant resource that explains about prayer and gives different simple ideas to pray that can be used anywhere and anytime of the day. It's pocket sized, so you can slip it into your pocket, or bag. You can get details by googling – www.trypraying.org and it is written by 'There is Hope'. Or you can download the 'trypraying' App.

Prayer is like having a conversation with God, you don't need special words or to have a particular body position or particular place to pray. It's amazing because we can pray anywhere, anytime and about anything. He is already there waiting in anticipation to hear us and chat to us.

As we said our goodbyes she recommended the best show to go and watch, which was one I would never have normally considered. But I had no idea, it was the show that both my husband and daughter really wanted to see but didn't want to say. And we managed to get 3 of the last few remaining tickets available for the sellout show.

Just as we had prayed before leaving the UK and whilst we were away that we would experience God's favour every hotel gave us complementary upgrades and gifts were left in our room. Throughout our holiday, God kept us safe. Even when someone tried to steal our underground pass, or when we were travelling on the underground late at night, we knew God's protection and care. It was like a wall or shield of protection that surrounded us wherever we went.

God is a God of beautiful surprises. He is able to do so much more than we dare ask or imagine. He can enable miracles to happen. Even when it seems there isn't any possibility or hope, He is able to do immeasurably and infinitely more than we can imagine!

We need to ask and trust Him. If He has created the world and everything to interact and fit together so perfectly, how could He not have even more perfect plans for you? He loves you, you are so precious to Him and He sees you as the apple of His eye.

Have you ever wondered what it would be like, if you asked Him to reveal who He really is and His character to you? For He is all loving, all trustworthy, super abundantly faithful and exceedingly good. The words that you read in this book only catch a glimpse of what He is like, as there is so much to discover. Just by spending a moment in His presence, you will be forever inspired.

I invite you to ask Him to reveal himself to you. To dare you to share your hopes and dreams with Him and catch a glimpse of His reply to you.

Miracles are God's way of showing us He is here!

Chapter 5
MIRACLES AND HEALING
God heals the big and the small

"And we can be confident that He will listen to us whenever we ask Him for anything in line with His will. And if we know He is listening when we make our requests, we can be sure that He will give us what we ask for"
1 John 5:14–15 NLT

The Bible encourages us to know, that we can always confidently talk to God and we can know that He is always listening. Whether we are young or old, He loves to hear us and it is always His will to heal us. He loves and cares for all of creation whether it is big or small.

For many years we had been thinking about having a puppy, and then the day finally came! We were travelling to collect her. She was the happiest and most enthusiastic Labradoodle you could ever meet.

She was a chocolate brown bundle of joy, brimming with enthusiasm and excited to meet people, to play and have fun. We laughed as we travelled to school one morning before we picked her up, as we wanted to give her a name that reflected her personality. As we 'googled' names that reflected the meaning joyful, we settled on calling her 'Bella', and her long name was 'Bella Jubilate!'

Finally, we arrived home, the afternoon flew by having fun playing with her and letting her explore her new home. Later in the evening we settled Bella into her crate with cozy blankets, however the first night was a rather noisy affair!

She was barking and howling most of the night, we were wondering if may be having a puppy was not such a great idea after all! We woke the following morning a little bleary eyed and my husband and daughter left early as they had tickets to watch 'The Open'.

Whilst they were out for the day, I chatted to God and asked Him how we could settle our new puppy, so that she didn't bark all night. I felt a sense that I should pray over the crate and area she slept in and asked that God's peace filled the space. As the day went on I continued to ask God if there was anything else I should do. I noticed that when I went out of the room she liked to sit and lie down by a white pair of slip-on shoes. That evening I placed the shoes by the side of her crate and prayed that she would sleep peacefully.

Wow it worked a treat!

My husband and daughter came home very late to discover our new puppy was as quiet as a mouse, fast asleep. Every night since then she has never woken us up barking, in fact she's so settled she often doesn't make a sound at the weekends until around 9.30/10am in the morning, which in 'doggie circles' is completely unheard of!

Completely bemused and surprised, by a quiet night's sleep my husband asked the following morning what I had done, to which I replied, I prayed! Little did we know we would pray another prayer which we would see answered before our very own eyes!

A few weeks later, we noticed that our puppy had a large growth on the inside of her ear. Unsure what it was, we took her to the vets. The veterinary surgeon immediately expressed concern as she was just 12 weeks old and growing rapidly, which in turn meant the lump potentially could grow quickly too. In addition to this she had concerns as initially there was no way of knowing if the growth was cancerous.

Immediately the veterinary surgeon recommended the best course of action would be to take some swabs of the area and send them off the laboratories for tests. As the results were going to take a few days to come back we were allowed to take Bella home and told to keep a close eye on her ear, checking to see if the growth grew any larger and to get in touch immediately if it did. She explained that depending on the size of the growth, they might need to operate, and if they did there was a chance it would affect her hearing, because of where the growth was situated.

As we drove home with Bella in the car we were in shock, tearful and upset to think our new little bundle of fluff was not well. We had waited such a long time before even having our own puppy and just in that short space of time she had become part of our family. We began to wonder if God could do something? Could God heal our dog? Is that something He could do?

We knew and had seen and heard of people who had been prayed for and God had healed them. Even all the accounts and stories in the Bible, where sick people were brought to Jesus, He healed every single one.

We thought we had nothing to lose by praying. So when we got home we placed our hands on our puppy's ear and prayed, asking that God would heal her. Praying and believing, the growth would completely disappear, so that there would be no need for an operation and her hearing would not be affected in anyway. We also asked some of our friends to pray too. Nothing happened straight away, but we left it in God's hands, trusting that somehow, He would heal her without the need of any medical intervention.

A few days later we spoke to the Vets and they said the growth wasn't cancerous and that they wanted to wait and assess her again in 3 to 4 weeks, to see if it grew any further. Then they would make a decision, as to whether to operate, or run further tests, but stressing there could be potential complications, as giving anesthetic to a puppy at such a young age wasn't a great idea. But either way, if the growth was removed, or remained, it still could potentially affect her hearing.

We continued to pray and believe for a miracle, that the growth would disappear. Sure enough within a couple of weeks, as we were routinely checking her ears we noticed the growth had completely gone! There was absolutely nothing there, no lump, no scar, it was as though nothing had ever happened. God had completely healed her. We took her back to the vets for a routine check-up and they were amazed that the growth had completely disappeared without any medical intervention and she still has perfect hearing.

To some reading this, you might wonder what an unusual thing to happen and do. Jesus wants us to know that He is the same today, yesterday and forever. He wants us to know and experience the extra-ordinary, because He can take us on extra-ordinary journeys. Like the tapestry of our lives we sometimes only see the back, or only certain coloured threads, however God longs to weave His colour and beauty, into our lives and those around us. So that we can walk in wonder of all that He can and is easily able to do and know that He loves us.

I wonder if you have a question or prayer that maybe seems big, or maybe small that you would like to ask God? Is there a 'thread' or something that you have always wondered? There is nothing too big or too small for God to do, or question too difficult to answer. He cares for all creation and all things, and He cares especially about YOU!

Miracles are God's way of showing us He is here!

Chapter 6
POWER OF A PROMISE AND POWER OF PRAISE
Freedom from fear

"May the God of hope fill you with all joy and peace as you trust in Him, so that you may overflow with hope by the power of the Holy Spirit"
Romans 15:13 (NIV)

It was a dream come true to visit South Africa. Just a few days earlier we had been on a safari with 'Thanda Safari', and stayed in a remote area of KwaZulu-Natal, where we were amazed and in awe of the beautiful and diverse country and the opportunity of seeing so many endangered animals in the wild. Each day we had gone out on a jeep with our tour guide. He often asked us what we would love to see and each and every time we were in awe of God's amazing creation.

One morning, just as the sun was rising before we left the lodge, we had prayed that we'd see a white rhino, which are really rare and we didn't just see one but eight, all standing together! Then later that day we prayed we'd see a female lion and saw ten lions, three adult lionesses and seven baby cubs, all together in a pack, sleeping and playing. We then asked our guide if there was a possibility of seeing a leopard, to which he said the only way that you might catch a glimpse of a leopard was if they found us. So, again we prayed that He would bring a leopard across our path and also asked God that we would see something that our guides had never seen before. As we drove down a dirt track we came across a female lioness and her three cubs which were no older than three weeks, and they walked casually past the jeep. The 'Look out' guide sitting on the front of the jeep was completely lost for words, as had never seen anything like this before! Our prayers continued to be answered as later in the day unusually a leopard didn't come to us but we found a leopard as were travelled down the dirt tracks as dusk approached. Again, the Game driver was lost for words, as neither he nor anyone else had seen a leopard for over two months! A double blessing!

A few days later we travelled further south to the Zambia and Zimbabwe boarder, to see one of the 'Wonders of the World', the Victoria Falls.

My husband suggested that as this was a once in a lifetime trip, we should see the Victoria Falls from different angles and perspectives. From The Gorge seeing and hearing the thunder and roar of the water flowing over the Falls, to being in the vibrant heart of the Falls swimming at the edge of the water. Also to experience the majestic and panoramic views airily from the sky, giving us a greater panorama of this amazing place that God had created.

Just those words 'up high' and 'being by the edge' made me a little tingly and scared and caused me to take a deep breath. However, immediately as my husband said this, I felt

God was saying He was giving me an opportunity to trust Him.

You may have guessed reading this, I had a fear of heights. I wonder if, you too, have a fear of something or have experienced fear?

I always had a fear of heights and often found even the thought of being at heights both scary and daunting. Generally, I was able to go to the top of high buildings, however I always had to look out onto the horizon and could never look down. On occasions where we visited spectacular vista points from places like the CN Tower in Toronto, or The Shard in London, I wouldn't be able to walk across the glass toughened floor which was often at the top of the buildings or even look through the glass panels where you could see the ground below. The idea of standing next to the safety barriers (even though they are safe), I would find terrifying. Just walking across The Gorge, which is a bridge that goes over part of the Victoria Falls made me anxious and gave me butterflies in my tummy, with fear.

However, I somehow knew God could and would use this opportunity to take away my fear of heights forever. But I needed to take a step of faith and trust Him completely. This was an opportunity to experience the beauty of the Victoria Falls and it was going to be a life changing experience too!

I want to encourage you that if you have something that you are fearful or anxious about, it doesn't have to stay that way. God delights in freeing us from our fears and allowing us freedom, so we can step into the fullness of everything He has for us. I pray that as you read this next chapter, you too will be inspired, that we don't need to live our lives in fear, but we can overflow with joy, hope and peace. It's a promise God has given to you, all you have to do is ask!

We have a very dear friend called Lois, who is like a mother to me and one of the friends who I often meet up with and we often pray together. We keep in touch by texting and sometimes by sharing prayers God has answered, or things to pray for. This was one of those occasions.

30th August - 18.45

"Dear Lois,
We're at the Victoria Falls, on the boarder of Zambia and Zimbabwe! It's absolutely amazing! The sound and the thunder of the water is unbelievably loud, as it roars

over the edge of The Falls. The power and the spray of the water powering over the edge is spectacular. We've seen Elephants roaming freely along the river bank. It's the most breathtaking sight.

Tony has arranged for us all to fly on a micro-lite tomorrow, just as the sun rises over the Victoria Falls. As you know, I've had a fear of heights for years and this is such a massive step of faith. Yesterday, as we walked on the bridge which goes over the Gorge by The Victoria falls, it seemed so high. I managed it, but had to walk in the middle of the bridge, holding my husband's hand, looking straight ahead into the horizon, not daring for one second to look down. Just doing this, I felt nervous and scared.

Micro-lites are small and can hold no more than two people at a time, the pilot and a passenger, which means we are all flying separately and they are open to the elements! This by itself seems daunting. I've been in a helicopter before, however I've always needed to hold my husband's hand and struggled to look down; This time he's not going to be there, as he will be on another micro-lite!

Over supper tonight, we have been chatting and saying that maybe I should pray and ask if God might be able to arrange for me to fly with a Christian pilot! In contrast our daughter isn't anxious at all, but is so excited and can't wait. Please can you pray for safety for us all, that I have courage and know God's overwhelming peace. That this is an opportunity where Jesus takes away all of my fear of heights.

It's funny Lois, over the last few days, before we even came to the Victoria Falls, a Bible verse and a picture keeps coming into my mind, of an eagle soaring in the sky. And the words 'soaring as on the wings of an eagle'. I wonder if this is how God sees this forthcoming flight on the micro-lite? That He wants me to see and experience things from a different perspective, one where there is no fear and having freedom to see these opportunities in a totally new way. Just like an eagle is able to rise above the storms and use them to propel itself to greater and higher heights, I too will be able to rise above my fears too."

Are there things you are fearful or anxious of?
Would you like a new aerial perspective?
....to spread out your wings....and fly!

99

30th August - 18.50

"Dear Tanya
Rebecca and I will pray for you tonight! Do not fear…
you have a spirit of power, love, and sound mind. God
will be with you and will be holding onto you. We will
pray for your safety and peace…that you will love it."

31st August - 5.00 am

The alarm goes, it's still dark outside, and it's just 5am.
This morning we are flying on a micro-lite!

Wow the words or the thought didn't faze me at all. I
had total peace, no butterflies in my tummy, no fear, just
completely calm.

I sat on the end of the bed, all ready to go and looked into
the mirror on the wall in our bedroom. I saw two rainbows
reflecting in the mirror, coming from the wall behind where
I was sitting. Slightly intrigued by this, as it was still dark
outside, I looked at the wall behind me. But to my surprise
there was nothing there, no rainbow or colours on the wall. I
then looked back into the mirror, thinking maybe it was my

imagination, but there it was again, the reflection of the two rainbows interlinking in the mirror. Again I looked behind, and there was nothing on the wall behind.

I sat on the edge of the bed and wondered about how I could possibly see two inter-linking rainbows. Then I heard God say, 'Just like there are two rainbows in the reflection of the mirror, I will be with you as you go up in the micro-lite. You don't need to be anxious or fearful, I will be with you!'

As we travelled to the aerodrome and also whilst we were waiting for the safety checks, I heard God again reminding me of Daniel in the Bible, who was an amazing man of prayer.

Even though he was thrown into a lion's den, with wild lions, God protected him by sending an angel to shut the lions mouths and there wasn't even a scratch on Daniel, because he had prayed and trusted God. I felt God remind me and say, "If I kept Daniel safe, I will keep you safe too!" Then, the words "The Spirit of The Lord gives fullness of joy and peace as you trust in Me", came immediately into my mind.

Prior to arriving at the aerodrome we had decided that if the flights went up one after the other, my husband would take the first flight, our daughter the second and I would be the third. This would mean we would see our daughter safely into the micro-lite and also our daughter would not be the first or last in the air, or the first or last to land.

To my surprise as we waited for the 4 micro-lites to land on the runway, we were told the names of the three pilots and discovered that one of them was a Christian Pilot. He was described as a senior microlight pilot and engineer, who 'loved to play in the clouds' and would be flying the second micro-lite. Our daughter would be flying with the Christian pilot.

I had such a sense of peace, I knew God was with me and was thrilled that Grace was flying with him.

Just as the sun was starting to rise, my husband was invited to get into the first micro-lite. The second micro-lite approached the runway and we were told that in actual fact, the Christian was flying the third plane. This meant that I, was actually going to fly with him. How could that be, other than God knew my earlier prayer and that something significant would happen.

Our daughter climbed in the second micro-lite, full of smiles and excited by what she might see. I then climbed into the third Micro-lite. Heiko the pilot, did the last minute checks and said it was the most beautiful, clear day with no wind, perfect for a smooth flight and stunning views of the sun rising over the Victoria Falls.

As we taxied down the runway I had an overwhelming peace. Heiko asked me where we were from and what had brought us to South Africa. I then explained we were on a special family holiday and also celebrating my birthday. Seeing the Victoria Falls and flying in a Micro-lite over the Falls was something we never, ever, dreamed or imagined we would do. And for me, it was a massive leap of faith and trust, as for many years I had such a fear of heights.

As we went up in the air, Heiko said to me, 'God wants you to be free of all fear. God loves you and all of us, with an overwhelming love. His perfect love casts out all fear, because in Him there is only love, and light!'. In my heart, and my mind, I knew that this was true and I prayed, and said to God, 'I trust you, and I know You love me. Thank you that you are here, and you will always be with me. Thank you that you love me so much that all fear has to go In Jesus Name. I don't need, or want to be frightened or fearful of heights anymore. You have created this amazing world and this opportunity, for me to experience your perfect love and peace.'

At that moment something shifted, and changed forever.

As we flew and went up in the air, in the micro-lite, I had such an overwhelming sense of God's peace, which I had never ever, experienced before and such sheer over-whelming joy! The views over the falls were spectacular, seeing how the Zambezi River zigzagged through the Victoria Falls. It was stunning! The thunder, power, and spray of the water going over Falls was breathtaking, like I have never seen, heard or experienced before.

Wow, I could look down with sheer delight and wonder. I felt so free and yet so safe, soaring in the sky. It felt like I was flying and soaring, on the wings of an eagle, just like the words and pictures, God had given me earlier in our holiday.

To see and experience from our aerial perspective, how powerful, and majestic the waterfalls were, the inlets and areas where there were multitudes of animals gathering along the Zambezi River, was breathtaking. The Hippos, Crocodiles, and Elephants felt so close, it was like being the zoom on a camera seeing everything so close and from a perspective you only ever see on documentaries.

As we played in the skies, we saw interlinking rainbows that followed us all the way. Just like the ones I had seen in the mirror earlier that morning, reminding me of God's promise, that He would be there every step of the way and He would keep us all safe. Even though there were handles on the micro-lite to hold onto during the flight, I was able to stretch my hands and arms out wide from the micro-lite and feel the wind through my fingers, as we flew through the sky. This was something I would never in a million years believe I would have been able to do, but I did, because God took away all my fear of heights. It was a miracle in every way!

Even as I write this now, I am completely lost in awe and wonder of the stunning world God has created and that He would use this amazing place to take away all fear of heights.

Part of his plan was to bring a Christian micro-lite pilot, all the way from Germany, to pray and speak of God's love as we flew over the Victoria Falls! How can that be? God's detail and how He works is so spectacular!

As I got off the micro-lite, I felt so light, and free, knowing that something very significant had happened and fear had lifted off me. God had taken me on an amazing new journey of trusting Him, knowing and receiving complete freedom from the fear of heights. I believe that, just as God has done this for me, He can also do this for you. He can set us free from fear, so that we can enjoy the fullness of everything!

You may be reading this and have a fear of heights, flying, enclosed spaces or even a fear of something else. Jesus can take your fear away and replace it with overwhelming peace, fullness of joy and abundant love. All you have to do is ask Him, believe and trust that He will. He just invites us to take a small step of faith to pray and trust Him (although to you that may seem like a gigantic step!). He is a loving Heavenly Father, who is like a coach standing on the side lines, cheering you on, celebrating and helping you.

An hour or so later we were back at the Victoria Falls, walking over the bridges that go over the Gorge there, but this time, it was totally different. I was free and able to walk across the Gorge without the need to hold my husband's hand. I could stand by the edge of the safety fence overlooking the Falls, without any fear or butterflies in my tummy. I was able to see and experience things in a way I had never experienced before. I was able to see the awe and wonder of this place, like a curtain had been raised and I was able to experience the fullness and beauty here for the very first time.

People came up to me saying, "Weren't you the lady at the aerodrome who was scared of heights?" To which I was able to joyfully reply, "Yes I was, but I now have no fear of heights, I am completely free of all fear! I now have freedom to look down into the Gorge, take photos and revel in the beauty of this place without being frightened. Jesus has taken away my fear of heights, it's truly amazing!"

I wonder if the picture of the eagle soaring above the storms is a picture for you too. The storms may be like the fears, worries, or challenges we can sometimes face. There is an invitation from your Heavenly Father to pray and trust Him that He will help you to rise above the fears, worries and challenges you face.

An interesting fact is that eagles know when a storm is approaching. They are un-worried by the challenge ahead and actually fly to a high place, and wait for the winds to come. Then when the storm comes, the eagles spread out their large wings, so the wind lifts the bird up. The current then allows the eagle to rise up to greater heights, so it soars and fly's high above the storm. The Eagle doesn't escape the storm, but instead, uses the storm to fly higher.

With Jesus, we too can use our challenges, fears and worries as opportunities to rise above situations. Through prayer we can ask Jesus to help us in everything that we do, not just in challenging times, but in our everyday lives. He wants us to soar and fly, in figurative terms and to enjoy the fullness of everything that He has for us. To take away our fears, or worries, so these obstacles aren't holding us back, but propel us into the abundance of everything that we were always meant to be and to do everything we were always meant to do.

The following day we had planned the third part of experiencing the panorama of the Victoria Falls before travelling back to the airport to fly home that lunchtime. Swimming at the edge of the Falls at sun rise, little did I know that again God was going to do another miracle and show us that He was with us!

1st September - 05.30am

It was another early start, 5.30am in the morning. We were walking through the hotel grounds to the boat jetty, to board a boat to go on an organised trip on the Zambezi river, to swim in one of the pools that were at the top of the edge of Victoria Falls.

Within our Hotel grounds there were zebras, giraffes and monkeys which roamed freely in the beautiful grounds. As we walked beside a small pond where crocodiles frequented, I tripped on the path, and fell, hitting my head on an enormous stone at the edge of the path. Blood was pouring down my face, but amazingly I was still conscious and no crocodiles could be seen anywhere in sight!

As I lay on the ground, I looked up to the sky. I was immediately drawn to some birds flying effortlessly in the sky and knew I should watch them and apply pressure to my head. At the same time, I knew Jesus could heal me as I had seen and heard it happen many times before at our church and had read lots of stories in the Bible of Jesus healing people. So I decided to pray and ask Him to stop the flow of blood. I then started to sing worship songs.

Amazingly those few minutes as I lay on the ground, no crocodiles, monkeys, or giraffes appeared! God was surely looking after me. A buggy soon arrived and I was whisked off to the Medical Room at the Hotel. Whilst we waited a short time for the paramedic to arrive, the security staff started to clean up the wound. They discovered it was a really deep cut, but couldn't understand why there wasn't more blood, saying it made no sense, for a wound so deep there should be more blood.

They asked what had happened and I said I was a Christian and believed in the power of prayer and that as I lay on the ground I prayed, asking God to stop the flow of blood and heal me. And then I sang songs of worship. They too believed in the power of prayer, but were surprised and puzzled by what they saw and couldn't understand how I wasn't unconscious. It made no sense.

The paramedic then arrived, made an assessment saying it was 0.5cm deep and would need four stitches; He explained it was really unusual that I hadn't passed out, because of the severity of the fall, explaining there was a possibility of infection and damage to my skull.

He said initially he would anaesthetize the area, but apologised if his hands were shaky. It wasn't because he was nervous, but that he was trying to give up cigarettes and it was often one of the side effects.

Totally unworried by this, I again prayed, asking that God would fill the paramedic with His peace and his hands would be completely steady, so he would be able to accurately perform the procedure.

As I lay on the medical bed, our daughter sent a text to friends asking them to join with us and pray, for healing and no infection. And also praying that this accident would not complicate our flight home just a couple of hours later.

As he disposed of the medical supplies he used he said he too was a Christian and again, God had called him and his family to work in Africa! We chatted and shared with him some of the amazing answers to prayer that God had demonstrated on our trip and how the day before He had taken away all fear of heights and I had such peace and overwhelming joy. I then asked him, if we could pray with him, 'In the Name of Jesus', that God would help him as he gave up cigarettes so he would have no side effects, shakes or withdrawal symptoms.

To my surprise when we came out of the surgery room and were sorting out the paperwork, our daughter showed me a text from a friend she had received whilst I was being seen by the paramedic.

Text at 06.40:-

"I will pray, tell her 'no weapon forged against her will prosper'. Jesus is by her side. The enemy wants to rob her joy…BUT he won't. Tell her to praise Jesus, this is for a purpose and God can turn everything to good. May be she will speak to someone who needs to hear about Jesus. I prayed against any infection and for speedy healing. That there will be no fear, just the Love of God."

How could my friend of known what to say, other than Jesus spoke to her. It was a miracle, there was far less blood. I was conscious and able to pray and Jesus spoke to her encouraging me to know that in all things God brings both opportunities and good out of all situations. If I hadn't fallen I would never have had the opportunity of meeting the people I spoke to, they would not have seen that God can answer prayer and still does miracles.

Within an hour we were travelling to the Zambian airport to fly home. As we checked in, we noticed the departure times had changed. Somehow we had an hour's delay, which must have been Heaven sent. God had already prepared a way, our flight was delayed by an hour. Then out of the blue, in the hustle and bustle of the departure area, which was even busier due to the delay, we found a quiet space upstairs in an empty travel lounge waiting area.

As we sat waiting for the plane to arrive, we were wondering how or if we would get home that day, as they had placed an enormous bandage on my head. Wondering if questions would be asked, and if they might stop me flying home. I knew somehow, God did have a plan in this.

And He did. God has the most amazing way of talking to us. God can speak to us in many ways. Sometimes He uses the things around us, something we see hear, or read.

As we waited for our aeroplane to arrive, I listened to a beautiful song based on the Psalm 23: 1-6. The words encourage us and very much speak of how God is like a shepherd or a best friend who is with us, in all situations, and circumstances.

"Yahweh is my best friend and my shepherd.
I always have more than enough.

He offers a resting place for me in his luxurious love.
His tracks take me to an oasis of peace near the quiet brook
of bliss.

That's where he restores and revives my life.
He opens before me the right path
And leads me along in his footsteps of righteousness
so that I can bring honor to his name.

Even when your path takes me through
the valley of deepest darkness;

fear will never conquer me, for you already have!
Your authority is my strength and my peace.
The comfort of your love takes away my fear.
I will never be lonely, for you ae near.

You become my delicious feast
even when my enemies dare to fight.
You anoint me with the fragrance of your Holy Spirit;
you give me all I can drink of you until my cup overflows.

So why would you fear the future?
Only goodness and tender love pursue me all the days of my
life.
Then afterward, when my life is through,
I'll return to your glorious presence to be forever with you!"

Psalm 23:1-6 The Passion Translation

As I listened to the words, they resonated with all that had happened on our holiday. The song was a picture of all the many blessings, and opportunities to trust Him, which had opened up for us on our holiday. He was reminding us that Jesus is our shepherd, who cares so deeply for us all. As a shepherd His purpose is to give life in all its fulness.

He had led and blessed us with the most amazing journey, with memories to treasure. Times where we trusted and knew His goodness and favour. He had led and blessed us with His luxurious love that conquers and casts out all fear giving us time together to have fun, relax and explore. Being surrounded by His perfect peace and experiencing overwhelming joy; Even here, in the unlikeliest of places, in a busy airport lounge, He provided a perfect quiet space, an oasis of peace with the softest lounge chairs to relax and wait, away from the busyness of the main departure area.

Then, just as the words of the song echoed the Bible words, that *'He opens before me the right path and leads me along in his footsteps of righteousness so that I can bring honor to his name'* (Psalm 23:3b TPT), our delayed plane landed on the runway. It was like God had been singing this song for us and to remind us that He was and will forever be always with us and He was now taking us safely home.

Waiting for the aeroplane and hearing the song, I had such an overwhelming sense of God's peace and I knew there would be no further complications. I knew it would all be ok, because I had a overwhelming peace, and joy, that ran deep, because I knew that God was able to do immeasurably more than I could ever dream possible.

Once we came home, the Doctors were amazed that I never had a headache, concussion or lost consciousness at any point. I had no infection or damage to my skull, and the stitches came out in record time!

As you have read this chapter I wonder if you have ever experienced a joy that runs deep and overflows? A peace that rises up and surrounds you in all situations and circumstances?

Often we try to satisfy our happiness ourselves, sometimes it can be fleeting or perhaps last for a while, but usually it's like a cul-de-sac, always looking for more. However true joy and peace does not have to be dependent on what our situations are, or what life is like. Knowing Jesus means that in all things and in all circumstances we can be confident that we will experience and stand in complete, abundant joy and overwhelming peace. A joy without limits overflowing; and a perfect peace which reassures and quietens your heart, guarding your heart and mind.

Every day Jesus wants you to experience and to have a life radiant with hope, one where every corner you come to and turn around it is full of opportunities and filled with rivers of joy. He wants you to know and experience a peace that weaves its way through our everyday lives. It's something we can ask Jesus for and is a promise for you (Romans 15:13).

Do you know joy and peace like this? It is there waiting for you. All you need to do is ask.

Chapter 7
PICTURES, SIGNS AND DREAMS
God can speak to us in many different and unexpected ways!

"When the Sprit of truth comes, He will guide you into all truth. He will not be presenting his own ideas; he will be telling you what he has heard. He will tell you about the future" John 16:13 NLT

Through our lives we meet lots of people. Some become friends or some may just be acquaintances.

Some people we get to know really well become loyal best friends, some are brutally honest friends, some are fearless adventurers and some are wise mentors. Others we know just by name or recognise by their face.

I wonder what sort of friends you have? I wonder, what would be your perfect way of spending time with your closest friends and how you love to talk them? How and what would you confide and share with them? Some friends you may ask for advice from, or share advise with. Some you have a laugh with and are great fun to be with.

Let's take a moment and think of one of these friends. On a scale of 1 to 10, where would that friend be on the scale? With '1' knowing not much more about them than their name and a '10' knowing them really well? I wonder why are they special? What makes them a great friend?

Wherever they are on the scale, our friends can play a part in inspiring us, standing with us and cheering us on. Friendships bring colour and vibrancy to how we see, live, and experience life. They can directly, indirectly, verbally, and non-verbally impact how we approach things and what we do.

Did you know that just as you have friendships, close friends and family, there is also a Heavenly Father who also longs and loves to have a close, special friendship with you? Just as you have friends you can trust, He too is someone whom you can trust. He loves to speak to you in many ways and take you on amazing adventures, both in your everyday life; and to see and do things that you would never dare dream possible.

So how do we know this? The Bible is full of so many promises that are for you. In Psalm 32:8 (NLT), it says

"The LORD says
'I will guide you along the best pathway for your life.
I will advise you and watch over you.'"

What an amazing thought, that there is someone who can and is able to guide us on the 'best pathway'. There is someone who is able to do immeasurably and infinitely more than we would ever dare ask or imagine. This someone is a Heavenly Father who has created you, knows and loves you because He wants friendship with you! He is forever seeking ways to catch your imagination and show you He is already here with you. He can do this because He knows you, He knows your comings and goings. He is there when you sleep, when you are awake, and wherever you go He is always there.

I wonder if you have ever thought of a friendship in this sort of way? I wonder if you have ever chatted or prayed to God and know Him personally from this perspective? I wonder if you know Him as the most special and amazing friend ever? I wonder on the scale of 1 to 10, how well you know Him? There is no right or wrong answer. Wherever you are on the scale, God longs to be more than just an acquaintance and for you to experience His unconditional love.

So how do we get to know Him? How do we know what He is saying? How does God speak to us?

God is a Heavenly Father who literally loves to speak to us. He is actually speaking to us all the time! Yes, it's true,

He is speaking all the time. He desires to speak to us and speaks in so many ways.

He often communicates with us using our senses, through all we see, hear, experience, taste and smell. Through music, things we read, pictures, dreams, creation, as we read the Bible, as we worship and pray. The list is endless!

Maybe you are reading this and have sometimes wondered, or asked the question, "Is God, really there? Or maybe, if God will really answer your prayers?" The answer is always, Yes. He is always there and He is always talking to us. However sometimes when He is speaking to us, we may not recognise His voice.

The Bible promises us that we can ask Him to help us to recognise when He is speaking to us, all we have to do is ask. Just as you spend time with acquaintances getting to know them, they can become a close friend. You begin to understand and know them better and 'know how they tick'. What they love and what they are like and you also become better at recognising their voice. In a similar way you can recognise God's voice as you spend time with Him.

The more you chat to God, the more you will easily recognise it's Him speaking to you. In a similar way, when you speak to someone on the phone you initially don't know very well, you may not recognise their voice straight away, however the more often you speak to them, the more quickly and easily, you recognise their voice.

So how can we chat to God and understand what He is saying to us? You can talk to your Heavenly Father, as you would a close friend. You can share with Him about your day, what's on your mind, what's going well, challenges, your greatest and happiest times, your fears and worries. You can take it all to Jesus in prayer. You can share absolutely anything with Him and He will not be surprised, or judge you. Then as you talk to him, leave a moment or a space to listen, to what He longs for you to hear. You could say a simple prayer like 'Holy Spirit, help me to catch or recognise what you are saying'.

When you 'listen' to God, it does not necessarily mean you will hear an audible voice, but often it can be an idea, a thought, a picture, or a word, that comes into your mind. It's like a 'light bulb moment' of revelation, that 'is perfect for that situation' and 'sits right'. It can make your spirit leap inside with excitement and peace, both at the same time.

There is an invitation for you today, wherever you are in your journey of knowing who Jesus is. Whether it is for the first time, or you know Him already as your Lord and Saviour.

I invite you to imagine you are standing on a beach and take a moment to chat to Jesus.

It is a beautiful sunny day the sun is shining down and you can feel the warmth of the sun. You are walking on the sand with bare feet.

Imagine what it feels like to be walking on the sand and have sand through your toes.

As you look down the beach, you can see the calm, crystal clear, sea gently coming in. The sea is like a picture of God's love. I wonder where you are on the beach? Are you sitting on the beach admiring the amazing view? Are you playing games on the beach? Are you walking along the sand, but your toes are not quite touching the sea gently coming in?

I wonder if you have stepped into the 'sea of God's love', which is gently coming in? Have you, or would you like to step in and accept His invitation to 'paddle' explore, to know Jesus? This may be for the first time, or maybe, you have known about Him for a long time but would like to know Him more.

He has created the world and all things, for you to enjoy. He loves you and longs for you to take a step of faith and know Him in a real and personal way. To know Him as your friend and Heavenly Father; to know and to experience the treasures of everything that He longs to share with you. Will you take that step into the water? You can step in, saying a simple prayer and ask Jesus to reveal himself to you and show you He is real. That He is there and you would like to experience His love.

For others, it may be asking to help you recognise when He is speaking to you and to hear what He is saying.

Like the water covers your feet, God also wants you to know and experience, His perfect love which He has for you. He wants to bless you with His love. That you know how wide, how long, how high, and how deep His love is. He wants you to know that you can literally wade into, and swim in the sea of His love. His love for you is so deep and unending!

Wherever you are in your journey of exploring and knowing Jesus, whether it is for the first time, or if you already know Him there is an invitation for us all to listen, and catch, the song He is singing back to us.

Why don't you take a moment....

- And tell Him how you feel and what's on your mind?
- Talk to Him about your friendship with Him.
- Ask Him what He would like to say to you?
- What does He most love about you and why?
- What is your response to Him?

If you would like to pray, and invite Jesus into your life, to be your friend and Saviour, there is a prayer you could use at the end of the next chapter 'Knowing Jesus - the greatest miracle of all'. You could use this prayer, or say your own prayer and accept His invitation, which is freely given for everyone.

I wonder what you chatted to God about? I wonder what His reply was to you?

We are only a moment from His presence.

I often chat to God throughout my day, sometimes silently in my mind, sometimes out loud. I love to spend time with God and listening to Him when I go for walks early in the morning. Often I will chat to God when I am doing the school run, or driving the car, or when I do jobs and errands. There is no place where we can go where we can't catch His beautiful voice!

More recently I have experienced and discovered that God can talk to us through dreams. I have read stories in the Bible of people who have had dreams and visions, which had very special and significant meanings. One example being Mary and Joseph. An angel appeared to Joseph in a dream telling him that his fiancé Mary would have a child, called Jesus, the Messiah.

The wise men too, had a dream. They followed a star in search of Jesus bringing gifts of gold, frankincense and myrrh, but were warned in a dream to go home another way.

We all have had dreams. Sometimes we discount them but sometimes our dreams are extraordinary signs and wonders of how God can sometimes speak to us. This next story is about a dream that was life changing and hopefully will inspire you to know that God can speak to us in significant ways, one of those being through dreams.

One Sunday morning I went to church. During the service they shared with us that as the prayer team gathered to pray before the service, as they listened to God, they sensed Him say there would be someone in the service who had problems with their neck and glands. They felt they should give an opportunity to invite that person to come forward for prayer and to pray for them, because Jesus was going to heal them.

At the time I was experiencing problems with my thyroid. I wasn't on medication, but was being monitored by my doctor as my thyroid levels were getting gradually worse. I was border line potentially requiring medication for the rest of my life. When this was shared in the service, I immediately knew it was an invitation for me to go forward for prayer.

Later that same week we had teaching led by Simon, one of the Ministers at our church about how the Holy Spirit speaks to us and that our Heavenly Father can speak to us in many ways. One of those ways can be when we are asleep, through our dreams. Up until this point when I prayed or worshipped, God often gave me pictures that He explained but I had never experienced Him speaking to me through a dream. So that evening I prayed with one of the church leaders that God would speak to me through dreams.

About a week later, on the Friday evening, I had a dinner party for some close friends from the Ablaze Prayer Team, I wasn't feeling very well throughout the evening, but we had a great time catching up. That night I went to bed and something unusual happened. For the first time God spoke to me in a dream! But this was not like a dream I had ever had before.

I don't know about you but sometimes I have had dreams and wake up and almost immediately forget them. Other times, I have remembered them for a while and then forget them, but this one was very different and still to this day, it is crystal clear. It was a significant dream with a miraculous outcome.

In the dream I saw a picture of a long wooden park bench, which was large enough for several people to sit on. As I looked at the bench, I heard a man say, "Come and sit with me, spend time with me. Come and sit on the bench, you can lean back on the bench. Just as you lean back on the bench, you can relax and lean back on me and trust my words and not your own understanding".

As I sat on the bench, next to this friendly looking person, I wondered who it was. The words He said seemed familiar, they were from Proverbs 3:5-6.

I then asked this man "Is that you Jesus? Are you here? Are you with me now?"

In a gentle voice, Jesus replied "Yes, it is! Its's good!"

Then, in the dream, as I sat on the bench with Jesus, He spoke to me and He prayed for me. As He prayed, He prayed and spoke promises from the Bible, for me over my life.

"Trust in the LORD with all your heart; do not depend on your own understanding. Seek his will in all you do and he will direct your paths" Proverbs 3:5-6 (NLT).

Rather than just saying the Bible verses, Jesus spoke lovingly and gently personalising the words saying, 'Tanya, Trust in the LORD with all your heart; do not depend on your own understanding. Seek my will in all you do, and I will direct your paths".

Then as we sat on the wooden bench chatting together, Jesus said "What is happening now in your life is good, and I am pleased". He spoke so many promises and words of encouragement. It was a life changing moment of realisation of how much He loved and knew me. Then Jesus placed His hands on my head and blessed me saying I was beautiful and wonderfully made; And He both preceded me and followed me. He then blessed, and spoke over all my organs in my body, telling them to work and function in perfect order, balance, and harmony".

The following morning I woke up and felt completely well. I felt as light as a feather, it was as though something significant had happened that night. Little did I know that as a result of the prayers Jesus prayed, my Thyroid was completely healed.

I continued to feel great. All of the symptoms that I had experienced which are often associated with thyroid problems had completely gone. For me the main ones being I always felt cold, even when it was warm and I had several layers of clothing on compared with everyone else and I always felt tired. But now I wasn't tired and felt warm! Hallelujah!

A few weeks after the dream my doctors contacted me for another routine blood test, to check my thyroid levels. But this time when the results came through they were completely normal, and have been ever since!

The doctors wanted to speak to me as the results didn't make any sense and wanted to run another blood test. Normally once your thyroid is being monitored the inevitable outcome is always medication for an over active or under active thyroid. Perplexed they asked what I had done and were lost for words that something like this could ever happen. It was a miracle and could not be explained in any other way! I had a dream like no other, where Jesus had prayed and healed me!

Our Heavenly Father loves to speaks to us in the most amazing and profound ways. When He speaks to us it is always good, it is always loving and it is always Biblical. Whenever He speaks it never contradicts His character or nature, because He is always loving, always trustworthy, always faithful and always good. This dream was a beautiful way in which I experienced His love and kindness, and it was like a meeting I had never, ever experienced before. This is something you can experience too, all you need to do is ask Him! Since then I have had many other dreams, each time if they have been for me or someone else they have been life changing dreams!

You may remember at the beginning of the book I briefly mentioned that the Holy Spirit inspired me to write this book. I thought I would share a little more about this, to encourage you how God sometimes speaks to us. It is an astonishing story and I am sure how God works will make you smile!

We had been back from our holiday in South Africa for about two weeks and my husband had been admitted into the tropical diseases unit in hospital and was in a private room as they weren't sure if he might have been contagious. The doctors had run lots of tests and were unsure as to what it might be, thinking he may have had a combination of shingles and possibly something else that he may have picked up on our holiday in South Africa. Perplexed and puzzled by this they continued to explore different options and they gave him antibiotics.

Each time my daughter and I went to visit my husband in hospital, we asked him if we could ask our friends at church to pray, that we might establish what the cause of the problem was. Initially he wasn't keen as he felt that God had far more important and significant things to do and he didn't think it was something we could ask God about. However my daughter and I knew this wasn't the case, as God loves us, and delights in answering our prayers. This was something He could easily do! However, on the Friday, out of desperation and knowing he would probably be in over the weekend, Tony finally agreed that I could speak to our worship team at church. So I sent a text asking them to pray.

Early the following morning, my friend Lois rang. She said she that as she had been praying, she felt God say to her that the reason my husband was unwell was because he had been bitten by a 'Tick', an 'African Tick'. Saying that often when hospitals do tests for African Tick fever, they have to send samples off to laboratories, and this in itself can mean the results can take a long time to come back.

Really excited I immediately rang my husband, and shared with him that Lois had been praying and as she chatted to God, the words that God said to her. To which he replied that it made lots of sense, as the day before the Consultant had mentioned they were going to run a number of other tests, one of which would take a long time to come back.

The next day, on the Sunday I was reading my Bible and praying. I felt God say to me that I would write a book, this book you are now reading. It was going to be a book about prayer and miracles. Immediately He gave me not only the ideas, but the detail of every chapter and who the book was for.

I had a strong sense it was going to be a book for both people who didn't know Jesus and also a book to encourage everyone to believe in the power of prayer. I knew it was going to be a short book, one that could be read in a few hours so it could be taken on journeys such as flights and trains. And it was a book that would be available in airports and train stations.

In addition to this as I was chatting to God and writing the details down, I also sensed that the book would be either written, or partly written, before my husband would come out of hospital.

The following day, on the Monday, I went to visit my husband in hospital. As I walked into his room he said the Consultant had been in to see him and some of the tests were back. The Consultant now thought he had a combination of shingles and being bitten by an African Tick! The medication for it was antibiotics.

Wow, that was what God had revealed to Lois just two days before! On the Tuesday morning Tony rang to say that he was going to be discharged from hospital and he would be able to come home with antibiotics. As soon as the medication had been prepared for him, he would be allowed to go.

As the morning went on, I was happily doing jobs around the house and every so often my husband would ring and say he'd still not received his medication. Each time he was getting more frustrated that it was taking so long.

This happened several times and I wondered whether the reason why his medication was being delayed was because God was waiting and waiting for me to start writing this book before he was dis-charged. Putting the thought to the back of my mind, I continued to do some more jobs, then I got another phone call to say the medication still wasn't ready!

This then made we wonder if what God had said to me two days before was in actual fact true! God had commissioned me to write this book and Tony wasn't going to be released from hospital until I had started to write. That couldn't possibly be true, could it?!? So I got my laptop out and the notes God had given me two days earlier and started to write the introduction to this book.

The phone rang again, the antibiotics still hadn't been done. Again my husband said "I really don't understand why this is taking so long!" I replied I think there may be a reason why there is a delay, but didn't like to say why. Wondering if God wanted me to write the introduction, before he was allowed to be discharged!

Then, just as I wrote the last sentence the phone went again. The antibiotics were ready! I realised and smiled, knowing that probably the reason for the delay was that God was wanting me to sit down and write the introduction.

Since then, God has clearly shown me the book would be published. He has given me a picture of walking with Jesus outside a large building and taking me inside to meet the publishers. Another person saw a picture of a book having wings, and being 'blocks of light', which were flying off the shelves. She described the blocks of light were the light of Jesus, shining His brightness.

I believe God speaks to everyone, there is no age barrier. He can guide us and inspire us in our everyday lives. He can help us understand and know His character and how lavishly He loves us. I encourage you, to take time to talk and listen to Him. To perhaps invite Him to speak to you, wherever you are and whatever you are doing. It may very simply start by sharing and telling Him about you day. Asking Him what He thinks of you, or what He loves most about you. You will be amazed by what He tells you and what He does. He is already waiting for you, all you need to do is take a moment to listen.

Why not do it now?

Chapter 8
THE GREATEST MIRACLE OF ALL
Knowing Jesus!

"For Anyone who calls on the name of the Lord will be saved"
Romans 10:13 NLT

The greatest miracle of all is knowing Jesus and to be given the gift of salvation.

We all have an invitation to know, see and experience the Greatness of God. God longs for us all not just to look through a single lens and "just live" our life on earth, but He longs for us to see and know Him as our Heavenly Father; to experience the fullness of life right now. How much He loves you, is thrilled with you and longs for you to know Him personally.

So how can we do this? How can we know Jesus? And how can we know Jesus like a friend?

For me, I was brought up in a Christian Home. My parents were Christians and we regularly went to church each week. I knew about God, but didn't know Him in a personal way, or know I could have a real, living, friendship with Him. This all changed when I went to a 'Youth For Christ' meeting, and heard that Jesus came into this world for me and for everyone.

The reason God sent His Son, Jesus, was that He created this world and wanted friendship with us. He loved us so much but us and the world we live in messed up. We call this 'sin'. The problem is, that sin separates us from God, because He is perfect in every way. People (us), try to fix things, or try and plug the gaps with relationships, good deeds, money, religion, alcohol etc. It may feel ok for a while but it doesn't fix the void, a bit like putting a round peg in a square hole, it doesn't quite fill the gap.

So, God sent His only Son, Jesus, who lived a perfect life and allowed Him to be killed on a cross, to pay for all the sin and brokenness. But that wasn't the end of God's perfect plan, because of God's amazing love and His genuine love for you and His desire for relationship with you and all people. Jesus rose from the grave to make a new life, "eternal life" possible for all of us.

Jesus told us that when we ask God to forgive us and believe in our hearts that (He) Jesus is the Messiah, the Son of God,   and that God raised Him (Jesus) from the dead, we will be saved.

So how do I do this? The Bible says in Romans 10: 9-10 (NLT):

"For if you confess with your mouth that Jesus is Lord and believe in your heart that God raised him from the dead, you will be saved. For it is by believing in your heart that you are made right with God, and it is by confessing with your mouth that you are saved"

By turning to God, asking Him to forgive us and believing and putting our trust in God, we can know eternal life. This is the most amazing miracle of all, as this means we can then come back into relationship with God, knowing Him as our Heavenly Father, receiving the gift of eternal life and the gift of Holy Spirit.

You might ask, who is the Holy Spirit? The Holy Spirit is our guarantee that we will have eternal life (Ephesians 1:13-14 and 2 Corinthians 5:5). Jesus said the Holy Spirit would come and be our guide and companion.

Very simply, if you want to do this now, you can say out loud a simple prayer to God. You could say something like this:

Lord Jesus, I want you to be my friend and Saviour. Thank you that you love me, and that you came into this world, died on the cross for me and rose again. I am sorry for all the things I have done wrong. Please forgive me I ask that you will be my friend and Saviour, and that you fill me with Your Holy Spirit. In Jesus Name. Amen.

If you have prayed this prayer, and/or would like to know more I'd encourage you to contact your local church or a Christian you know and tell them about what you have done. They will encourage you in your journey of getting to know Jesus.

This is just the beginning of an amazing and exciting friendship with Jesus and experiencing life in all its fullness.

The Living Water

An invitation to know Jesus...

Come to Jesus
He's the Living Water
He will satisfy your soul
Come to Jesus
His love abundantly flows

For He is life everlasting
He brings life and light to everything
Come to Jesus, the Living Water
For He will satisfy your soul

To know Him, is to receive Him
And believe He is Lord
For He shows endless mercy
And forgave and redeemed us all

BRIDGE

There's an invitation to know Jesus
He's living and He's real
Will you accept the invitation to know Jesus
He's waiting for your call

Will you receive the invitation to know Jesus
He's living and He's real
He's waiting for you call

Will you trust the invitation to know Jesus
It's within easy reach
He's waiting for your call

RESPONSE

Yes, I receive Your invitation Jesus
Your mercy never fails
For You are Jesus, The Messiah
Forgiving me and all who call
I will trust in You, Jesus
For You are the Saviour of the world
Fill me with Your Spirit, Jesus
I accept Your invitation now!

Miracles are God's way of showing us He is here!

Chapter 9
SO WHERE NOW?
'Every little miracle points to our Heavenly Father'

God can do infinitely more than we would ever dare ask or imagine!

There is an invitation for you from your Heavenly Father....He invites you to go on an extra-ordinary journey, where you will see and experience all that He has for you.

In every miracle, sign and wonder, and in everything He says and does it is like a 'ribbon of love', He has woven through for you. He wants you to see and know the 'bigness and greatness' of who He is.

He has a genuine deep love for you and cherishes you, as His son or daughter; And He is easily, able to do what seems impossible to us. He longs for us to be fully aware of His blessings and promises. To know and experience the fullness of His lavish love and unending grace. He wants us to know miracles can and do happen when we pray and speak out His promises.

So where now?

I, like yourself, am on a journey with my Heavenly Father. These are a couple of ideas that you might find helpful to encourage you as you pray, believing, trusting, seeing and experiencing the extra-ordinary journey with Jesus.

Ask the Holy Spirit to help you:

Firstly, as you pray, ask the Holy Spirit to help you to recognise more and more clearly, what delights and treasures He is sharing with you. Enabling you to have your eyes wide open, to see all God wants you to see and the fullness of everything He has for you.

Asking that He will enable you to understand and experience, the width, length, height and depth of God's love. That this love propels you as you pray and the Holy Spirit shows you how, and what, to pray.

Search The Bible for the promises He has already declared for you, in the situations you face and for those around you. Check out different translations (for example the NIV, Amplified Bible, New Living Translation, The Passion Translation or The Message Translations of The Bible) as they often help us to have a fuller understanding of what God is saying. The Bible App is a brilliant tool to do this.

For example, if you have some important decisions to make and need guidance you could look up and pray Jeremiah 29:11 (NLT),

"'For I know the plans I have for you", says the LORD.
"They are plans for good and not disaster,
to give you a future and a hope"'

ou could pray a prayer like this…

Heavenly Father, I thank you that the Bible, Your Living Word, promises that You have good plans for me and not disaster. Your plans promise a hope and a future. I ask that You will reveal and make clear what I should do about…………….. In Jesus Name. Amen

Prayer Journal:

Secondly, a note book or diary that you can use as a prayer journal is an amazing way to journey in prayer. As you pray you could write prayers into a note book, and create a prayer journal or diary. This could be simple notes, or a picture of something you are praying about. Children too, love drawing pictures of their prayers to God!

You could use this as a focus to help you pray and write the Bible promise next to your prayers. Then as God answers those prayers, write beside them what God has done, or a smiley face. Then thank God and share with others what has happened. If you prefer technology, you could do a similar thing on your mobile phone and even put reminders on it for you to pray about something.

If you are a more visual, tactile, or kinesthetic person, you could create a 'prayer jar'. Each time you pray a prayer you could place something in the jar to remind you what you have prayed, or you could write a prayer onto a piece of paper and place it in the jar. When the prayer is answered, you could then put it into a bowl or another jar. This will become a visual way to remember and thank your Heavenly Father for all He has done.

If you follow any of these ideas, or even something else that works for you, it is a really wonderful way of being encouraged and encouraging others in believing in the power of prayer. It also develops a heart of thankfulness as you remember and count your blessings. You will know beyond doubt, that your Heavenly Father is always faithful and forever good, in all situations and circumstances.

Gathering with other Christians to Pray:

Thirdly, gathering with other Christians and / or having a prayer partner to pray with, is a wonderful opportunity to share and encourage each other with what God has done.

There is also something very special that happens, when we pray in agreement with other people. It's like an added weight to our prayers when we pray together with other Christian's.

In Conclusion

In our ordinary lives God can and does do extra-ordinary things. He uses all people to demonstrate His amazing, extraordinary endless, never ending love. Our Heavenly Father's thoughts are far beyond anything we could think was possible, His ways are higher, more perfect and greater than we could even begin to ask or imagine.

God wants us to look, not just through a single lens, but to see the majesty and greatness of who He is, how He loves you and is so thrilled with each and every one of us. Having heavenly perspectives, being inspired by the Holy Spirit.

Like a tapestry we sometimes only see the back, but God wants us to see the front, the bigger picture of everything He has for us. So we can celebrate and know the beauty of all that He has done and enjoy the fullness of everything He longs to fulfil. Everyday we can walk in the wonder of all He is easily able to do in our lives and the lives of those around us.

I pray that as you've read this book, that you have been and will continue to be inspired, that our Heavenly Father really can do over and above more than we can dream or imagine! He says He is able to do super abundantly, and infinitely more, than we ever dare ask or imagine. This is His character and it is full of love.

Do you want to enjoy the fullness of everything He has for you?

Let's pray, and ask God to help us pray His 'God sized dreams'. Expecting Him to fulfil them superabundantly and giving Him all the glory, honour and praise!

"My thoughts are completely different from yours" says the LORD. *"And my **ways are far beyond anything you could imagine.***

For just as the heavens are higher than the earth, so are my ways higher than your ways and my thoughts higher than your thoughts.

*The rain and snow come down from the heavens and stay on the ground to water the earth. They cause the grain to grow, producing seed for the farmer and bread for the hungry. **It is the same with my word. I send it out, and it always produces fruit. It will accomplish all I want it to, and it will prosper everywhere I send it.***

You will live in joy and peace.
The mountains and the hills will burst into song, and the trees of the field will clap their hands.

*Where there were thorns, cypress trees will grow. Where briers grew, myrtles will sprout up. **This miracle will bring honour to the LORD's name; it will be an everlasting sign of his power and love."** Isaiah 55:8-13 (NLT)*